befo

D0298697

OXFORD TELEVISION STUDIES

General Editors **Charlotte Brunsdon**
John Caughie

British Youth Television

Feminist Television Criticism: A Reader
edited by Charlotte Brunsdon, Julie D'Acci, and Lynn Spigel

The Feminist, the Housewife, and the Soap Opera
Charlotte Brunsdon

British Television: A Reader
edited by Edward Buscombe

Television Drama
Realism, Modernism, and British Culture
John Caughie

Critical Ideas in Television Studies
John Corner

The Intimate Screen
Early British Television Drama
Jason Jacobs

Television and New Media Audiences
Ellen Seiter

British Youth Television

Cynicism and Enchantment

Karen Lury

CLARENDON PRESS · OXFORD

OXFORD
UNIVERSITY PRESS

Great Clarendon Street, Oxford OX2 6DP
Oxford University Press is a department of the University of Oxford.
It furthers the University's objective of excellence in research, scholarship,
and education by publishing worldwide in
Oxford New York

Athens Auckland Bangkok Bogotá Buenos Aires Calcutta
Cape Town Chennai Dar es Salaam Delhi Florence Hong Kong Istanbul
Karachi Kuala Lumpur Madrid Melbourne Mexico City Mumbai
Nairobi Paris São Paulo Shanghai Singapore Taipei Tokyo Toronto Warsaw
and associated companies in Berlin Ibadan

Oxford is a registered trade mark of Oxford University Press
in the UK and certain other countries

Published in the United States
by Oxford University Press Inc., New York

British Library Cataloguing in Publication Data
Data available

Library of Congress Cataloging in Publication Data
Data available

ISBN 0–19–815970–6

1 3 5 7 9 10 8 6 4 2

Typeset by Graphicraft Limited, Hong Kong
Printed in Great Britain
on acid-free paper by
T.J. International Ltd,
Padstow, Cornwall

Oxford Television Studies

General Editors
Charlotte Brunsdon and **John Caughie**

OXFORD TELEVISION STUDIES offers international authors—
both established and emerging—an opportunity to reflect on
particular problems of history, theory, and criticism which
are specific to television and which are central to its critical understanding. The perspective of the series will be international, while
respecting the peculiarities of the national; it will be historical, without proposing simple histories; and it will be grounded in the analysis
of programmes and genres. The series is intended to be founda-
tional without being introductory or routine, facilitating clearly
focused critical reflection and engaging a range of debates, topics,
and approaches which will offer a basis for the development of television studies.

Acknowledgements

THIS is a project that could not have been completed without the support of many people. I would like to thank John Corner for his consistent encouragement and rigorous thinking, John Caughie for his blunt but constructive editing, and Simon Frith for his enthusiasm and ruthless approach to some of my weaker arguments. I would also like to thank my friends and colleagues at Liverpool University, particularly everyone associated with the Institute of Popular Music.

I would also like to thank my sister, Celia, who does not guess how much she inspires me, and Tim Niel, who emerged, unsurprisingly, as an exacting and thoughtful proof reader.

In many ways this has largely been a family affair. It is appropriate therefore to dedicate this book to my mother, Toni Lury. Her curiosity and original approach to the world of ideas, as well as her unfailing emotional support, achieved far more than this book could ever represent.

Contents

1

Generation X
The 'Future of Television'

IN this book, I will be looking at British youth and British television, focusing on the late 1980s and early 1990s phenomenon
of British 'Youth Television', looking at programmes produced for
the Def II strand and elsewhere on the BBC, as well as programmes
either imported or produced specifically for youth on MTV and
Channel 4. During this period, different youth programmes established an aesthetic that has made a significant impact on the style of
many different television programmes, and in the production practices of certain programme makers working within British television
today.

The programmes are also revealing about the young people they
were intended to address; while they were not *reflective* of young
people—I will not suggest, for example, that the programmes were
truly representative of young people as they actually were—the
programmes were operational in that they encouraged a specific
way of coping with the various demands, pressures, and excitements
experienced by this generation of television viewers.

In the chapters that follow I will be looking in detail at programmes
and performers; before I do so, I want to identify the parameters of
this book and to point to the contradictions inherent in my study.
While it will become clear that 'youth' and 'television' as lived experiences and as social or theoretical constructs are often understood as
being very different, and even antipathetic to one another, my intent
is to indicate how a generation of youth—the so-called 'Generation X' (who were the post-boomer/ 'baby-bust' generation born in
the late 1960s and 1970s)—and a series of different television programmes (produced during a specific time period between 1987
and 1995) coincided. This coincidence encouraged an aesthetic
sensibility that combined 'cynicism and enchantment'. This meant
that although they were 'not going to be taken for suckers', young
people continued to invest in the pleasures and places produced by
television.

The coincidence of programmes and audience was enabled by a
particular combination of social, economic, and cultural factors:

factors which provided a living environment that was significantly different from that experienced by previous generations of youth. This necessarily affected all aspects of these young people's lives whether it was in their experience of employment; in the structure of their leisure time; in their attitude to the presence and pervasiveness of the commodity in their lives; in their relationship to past youth cultures; or most significantly, in their familiarity with, and of, different technological media.

How is this context to be understood? How did these factors determine the experience of young people, and how were they negotiated by the young people themselves? Undeniably, these factors and the changes they represented coalesce—but are not necessarily coherent—within the concept of 'post-modern culture', or should be acknowledged as symptomatic within society's post-modern 'condition'.

While some critics have already attempted to establish a link between post-modernism and youth, and post-modernism and television (and often, television specifically addressed to youth)[1] I want to distance myself from this work; indeed some of these studies have already been authoritatively critiqued elsewhere.[2] Nevertheless, whatever limitations there may be, an interpretation of contemporary popular culture as post-modern will be central to my argument. To this end, I will outline how and why such a perspective can be made viable, and highlight which characteristics of the post-modern will be drawn upon and explored in greater detail.

Much has been written about post-modernism and discussions have emerged from within a variety of disciplines; ranging from (and not exclusive to) literary theory, film studies, anthropology, science, geography, and history.[3] Understandably, it has appeared as a surprisingly diverse series of traits and practices that define various different aspects of the culture, economy, and social relations of contemporary society. As a mode, trend, or style, post-modernism has been characterized in several different forms: featuring as a cultural context, as an aesthetic, a condition, or a critical approach.

What links all of these forms is the way in which post-modernism is seen to produce a particular series of effects within each different sphere. Three of the most commonly cited, or prominent effects,

---

1 See John Fiske, *Television Culture* (London: Routledge, 1987), and E. Ann Kaplan, *Rocking Around the Clock: Music Television, Postmodernism and Consumer Culture* (London: Methuen, 1987).

2 See Andrew Goodwin, *Dancing in the Distraction Factory: Music, Television and Popular Culture* (Bloomington, Ind., and Minneapolis: University of Minnesota Press, 1992).

3 See, for example, C. Jencks (ed.), *The Post-Modern Reader* (London: Academy Editions, 1992).

are as follows: firstly, post-modern culture is distinguished by an annihilation of artistic 'difference' (particularly in the distinction between 'high' and 'low' arts, and between high or mass culture). Secondly, both in the writing of fiction and in the writing of history, post-modernism encourages the abandonment of both 'meta-' and/or 'grand' narratives (a change which is often presented as the replacement of one 'History' with many, or plural 'histories'). This means that traditional hierarchies in art, culture, and knowledge have been eroded, and superseded by a situation where individuals in a post-modern context are forced to accept a cultural milieu that is destabilized: one that is constantly shifting, temporary, and contingent. Thirdly, all of these factors are seen to have implications at an intimate or personal level; indeed, they seem to encourage a decentring of subjectivity, which in turn, implies the collapse of a coherent identity, so that identities are no longer fixed, or stable, but in process, or flux.

On a different level, economic changes, related to post-Fordism or post-industrialism, have also been related to post-modernism as they create flexible, casual working practices that have destabilized the traditions of mass production and mass consumption.[4] Such changes have also broken up the coherence of many job or career structures. With a subsequent decrease in job security, these economic factors have social and personal effects that also lead to the decentring of subjectivity noted above, and to an increase of uncertainty, as the enforced flexibility of working practices and the increasing power of transnational corporations destroy older relationships between individuals and their employers, and, potentially, certain individuals' perception of themselves as citizens in relation to specific nation states, or as permanent members of traditional communities. One further consequence of this is that, as old loyalties and certainties break down, 'other' voices, practices, and beliefs may take their place, or at least be revealed to be as valid or viable as any other belief or practice. This promotes a context where all truth claims, priorities, and perspectives are understood to be susceptible to change. As a result of economic, personal, and social instability, the successful negotiation of post-modern life is therefore associated with the ability to tolerate fragmentation, disjunction, and chaos. This may also be associated with the development of a kind of nomadic mobility, whether it be the flexibility required in order to move and change jobs, or the ability to take on, or adopt, different identities. It is a central part of my argument that the experiences and practice of the generation of youth under consideration would suggest that

---

4 This argument is explored in detail in David Harvey, *The Condition of Postmodernity* (Oxford: Basil Blackwell, 1989).

Generation X, or the 'baby-busters', are taking such negotiations to heart. This may, for example, take the form of rejecting traditional career paths, and lead instead to what appear to be abrupt changes of life-plans. And it is possible to see this in practice; for example, in his study of Generation X at work, David Cannon notes the surprise of older managers at the activities of their younger employees:

> At work a star performer can tell their supervisor in an annual review that all is well, and that they are committed long term to the company, only to return to their desk 10 minutes later to rework their CV or take a call from a headhunter. Managers are surprised and often hurt when their best employees suddenly announce they are unhappy and leaving to do an MBA or take a trip to New Zealand.[5]

Such abrupt changes may appear to older managers as dishonest and incomprehensible, but, for a privileged part of this youth generation, such decisions, along with a greater emphasis on the gaining of specialized knowledge outwith the workplace, reveal that some young people have begun to adapt to the insecurity of the job market by no longer valuing long-term career prospects. They prefer instead to create themselves as autonomous, experienced, and multi-skilled individuals. The flip side to this, however, for those young people who are not 'star employees', or for those who are unable to fund such major life changes as foreign trips, or further education courses, will not be so idyllic. Their career prospects may simply lead to a situation in which they are trapped into a series of low paid, low prestige jobs (what Douglas Coupland calls 'McJobs'[6]). Unsurprisingly, this kind of situation can provoke a behaviour pattern that encourages or exhibits a form of terminal apathy; hence a popular and negative sobriquet for this generation—'slackers'. Yet it is evident from popular reports that even this depressed group may determine for themselves a form of validation as they go about the business of acquiring particular forms of knowledge, or in their adherence to, and construction of, elaborate, and often antipathetic, lifestyles; witness the intensity and specialized knowledge of the dance/rave scene, and the defiantly unconventional lifestyle of the 'crustie'.[7]

In addition to the mutability of lifestyles, there is another key feature of post-modern texts and post-modern culture that ties

---

5 David Cannon, 'Generation X and the New Work Ethic', a Demos working paper (London: Demos, 1994), 9.

6 See Douglas Coupland, *Generation X: Tales for an Accelerated Culture* (London: Abacus, 1991).

7 See Sarah Thornton, *Club Cultures: Music, Media and Sub-Cultural Capital* (Cambridge: Polity Press, 1995), and Tracey Skelton and Gill Valentine (eds.), *Cool Places:Geographies of Youth Cultures* (London: Routledge, 1998) for some work on these different lifestyles.

them closely to the experience of this generation of youth; this is the concept and practice of commodification. The celebration of mass culture—with its reliance on, and association with, mass production —along with the co-option of high culture into popular arenas and forms, has led to the perception of an increasing 'commodification of culture' within post-modernism. It is suggested that commodification (and therefore post-modernism) offers a potential threat to genuine expression, as it is seen to lead, inevitably, to a homogenization of cultures and identities. As larger and larger communities buy in to the same aspirations, forms of expression, and lifestyle, real diversity is eroded as cultures are increasingly determined by a series of identical products that are marketed and consumed on a mass scale.

Mass culture and its associated commodification has long been critiqued within numerous discussions of modernity,[8] and it is mass consumption in particular that is seen to allow for, or facilitate, the emotional and ideological domination of large parts of the population by determining and even degrading their tastes and desires. The pleasures that commodities proffer are argued to be deceptive, illusory, and 'fake' as opposed to the real or genuine pleasures provided by the older, traditional forms of an authentically popular, 'folk' culture. What is significant about these arguments, within this context, is that they frequently appear in relation to negative assessments of contemporary youth's apparent obsession with labels, brands, and commodities, as well as their supposedly dubious over-familiarity with trivial or debased forms of culture—such as television or computer games. Here, for example, is a playful version of such an argument neatly summed up in Douglas Coupland's novel/treatise *Generation X*:

> **CLIQUE MAINTENANCE:** The need of one generation to see the generation following it as deficient so as to bolster its own collective ego: '*Kids today do nothing. They're so apathetic. We used to go out and protest. All they do is shop and complain.*'[9]

Whilst apocryphal and ironic, Coupland demonstrates that there is a more damning evaluation of Generation X in circulation than that provided by David Cannon's analysis, where it is argued that brands, and specialized knowledge of particular commodities, are exchanged between young people as a new form of communication and self-definition. Yet it is this latter perspective that is more in tune with the evangelical tone of Paul Willis, writing in a report emerging from the wide-ranging Gulbenkian inquiry on the cultural activities of young

8 The classic essay here is Theodor Adorno and Max Horkheimer, 'The Culture Industry: Enlightenment as Mass Deception', repr. In T. W. Adorno, *The Culture Industry: Selected Essays on Mass Culture*, ed. J. M. Bernstein (London: Routledge, 1991).

9 Coupland, *Generation X*, 21.

people. In the introduction to the report's findings, Willis argues that, rather than being dominated or brainwashed by a culture of consumption, the market and the commodities it offers provide the one arena in which young people may empower themselves:

> For young people it is not the commercialisation and commodification of culture *per se* which is the problem. On the contrary, it is clear that the market has been a liberating factor in the extension of the cultural resources for many young people. In fact young people have a creative role in shaping the contours of commercial culture in ways that are quite forbidden to them within 'official cultures'—education, literature, the arts—where the combined forces of privilege, class and the state too often reduce young people to powerless subjects. On the contrary, the market defines the geography of young people's culture. It is that world which they are taking over, transforming, and turning into real youth art.[10]

Although Willis's interpretation of young people and the market will bear some relation to the argument I will go on to make, his conclusions are more optimistic, and confined by a dated conception of the significance of certain power relationships. Whilst these relationships still exist, they have had to adapt to the contingency and fragmentation of a post-modern culture. In particular his assessment is hampered by his wish to promote the cultural 'resistance' of young people and the urge to celebrate their activities as a form of 'youth art'. A conclusion, I suspect, that is inappropriate or irrelevant to any of the outcomes imagined by young people themselves. Nevertheless, it does represent a change in the perception of what a commodity culture actually means, and how effective it is in determining the tastes and pleasures of individuals.

As an alternative, or as a development of Willis's arguments, I argue that shopping and knowledge about consumer products has a different kind of status within a society that is in some sense *defined* by the commodity. For Generation X, commodities, brands, and labels are inextricably bound into the most personal and intimate of practices, as well as those that take place on a wider social or economic scale. This cultural and economic shift is not so much a break from, or subversion of, modernity and modern consumption, but rather the effect of an accumulation and acceleration of tendencies already at work within the culture. In many Western societies, individuals within them can no longer be perceived as somehow separate from, and therefore potentially subject to, the 'thrall' of the alienating practices of the market; instead they are engaged in a more symbiotic

---

10 Paul Willis, *Moving Culture* (London: Calouste Gulbenkian Foundation, 1990), 12.

series of relationships with commodities. For Generation X, commodities are no longer always, or inevitably, perverting and distracting them from their real pleasures and needs. Rather, it becomes harder and harder to distinguish real or authentic desires from inauthentic pleasures and more and more difficult for individuals to envisage themselves as somehow outside of belief systems, practices, and living environments that are not also commodities, or that have not already been mediated in some way.

Jim Collins, in his discussion of post-modern culture, is able to dismiss as irrelevant the negative connotations associated with the previous conceptions of the commodity and consumer culture. He suggests, in relation to both popular and post-modern texts, that such arguments are riddled with an unnecessary nostalgia for a past 'Golden Age'.

> The commodity status of both popular and Post-Modernist texts appears to be their 'original sin' . . . that which makes them inferior works of art, somehow tainted by the filthy lucre one must pay in order to appreciate them. The foundation of this, of course, is a nostalgia for a Golden Age of 'folk' culture.[11]

He then goes on to argue that negative assessments concerning the threat of commodification also fail to recognize that the inherent lack of orchestration in post-modern culture will effectively work against or destabilize any potential homogenization of tastes and desires. He suggests that, while:

> We may indeed be constantly encouraged to define ourselves through commodities . . . the absence of co-ordination in such a process results in our being asked to define ourselves in quite different ways, thereby producing anything but a uniform subjectivity.[12]

This lack of co-ordination in post-modern culture may mean, in contradistinction to more conservative evaluations, that individuals will actually have a greater opportunity to determine their own consumption patterns than previously. As a consequence of this, the potential for mass conformity or for a uniform subjectivity may be in fact less certain than before. However, I would like to add that it is also important to note that although in theory there is freedom of choice within a commodity culture, such choices, developed as consumer practices, will continue to be marked by the divisions of class, race, age, gender, and wealth. Yet, whilst acknowledging that not all people have the

---

11 Jim Collins, 'Post-Modernism as Culmination: The Aesthetic Politics of Decentred Cultures' (1989), in Jencks (ed.), *The Post-Modern Reader*, 101.

12 Ibid., 104.

same kinds of 'symbiotic relations' with the same commodities, it is still fair to argue that since young people have had a significant impact on, and continue to exhibit an especially close relationship to, the market, their position in relation to global changes in consumption must be significant. Indeed, even during the boom–bust economic cycle of the late 1980s and early 1990s, they continued to have a higher disposable income than other parts of the population, along with a greater licence to experiment. Generation X is therefore very closely bound into the changes I have related above.

The flexibility, extremes, and fluctuations that this post-modern culture instigated are as a 'way of being' also closely associated with the category of 'youth' as a biological or transitional phase. This seems to be especially true when young people are understood to be going through a distinctive life-stage. Johan Fornas, in his book *Cultural Theory & Late Modernity* outlines why and how such tendencies have been established and are emphasized within the context I have outlined. Fornas writes that:

> The flexibility and mobility of youth lie deeply in modern society. Youth is in most epochs and classes a changing life phase and a category that is particularly sensitive to social transformations. This does not make all teenagers more radical or flexible, politically, socially or even stylistically . . . They can be reactionary conventionalists, but it is no coincidence that they form radical avantgardes of many kinds in a more visible way than most other age-groups. Even then, they continue to live in a state of inner and outer flux, of rapid transformations not only of the kind that we all experience in modern times and other periods of transition, but also in their very bodies and minds as well as in their social conditions.[13]

If youth was and continues to be associated with states of 'inner and outer flux' as well as being susceptible to 'rapid transformations', it is not difficult to see that, of all groups in society, young people may be particularly likely to take on and adapt to the contingencies and changes instigated by a post-modern culture.

At this point it is necessary to acknowledge that the definition of post-modernism I have been working with is limited, and possibly not representative of post-modernism at all. Indeed, it might be that it should be related instead to the culture of '*late* modernity'—a definition with which Fornas, for example, is certainly more comfortable. This slippage between the two terms late modernity and post-modernity in my discussion so far is exacerbated by the way in

---

13 Johan Fornas, *Cultural Theory & Late Modernity* (London: Sage, 1995), 244.

which I have implied that the changes I am discussing are not so much a break from the past—from 'modernity'—but are in fact the result of a speed up and an accumulation of practices that can be discerned within modernity itself. The fault, however, lies with the very openness and flexibility of the term post-modernity. As a concept, post-modernism embraces the confusion of the modern age in a way that either, as some critics would argue, establishes a break from modernity and its aesthetics and economics (hence 'post-') or, as is made explicit in other definitions, is to be understood as a 'new type of crisis *of* modernity itself'. Andreas Huyssen, for example, concentrates on the latter definition:

> Post-modernism at its deepest level represents not just another crisis within the perpetual cycle of boom and bust, exhaustion and renewal, which has characterised the trajectory of modernist culture. It rather represents a new type of crisis *of* that modernist culture itself.[14]

In support of this definition, Collins suggests that what is radical or different about post-modernism is not that it establishes a break from, or engenders the disappearance of, modernity and modern ways of life; rather that post-modernism demonstrates an embracing quality that allows for a synchronicity of opposing forms, styles, beliefs, and identities.

> What differentiates Post-Modernism from earlier periods is that while a specific style may be identifiable, its circulation and popularity do not define what is distinctive about the period. In other words, there is indeed a Post-Modernist textual *practice* in literature, film and architecture, etc., but what distinguishes the Post-Modernist context is the simultaneous presence of that style along with Modernist, pre-Modernist and non-Modernist styles—all enjoying significant degrees of popularity with different audiences and institutions within a specific culture.[15]

For critics such as Collins, the context of post-modernism is not a break from, or a comprehensive sub-version of, modernity, but a 'new type of crisis' or a re-evaluation of changes within modernity.

If some definitions of post-modernism and the tendencies associated with 'late modernity' can be argued to be so similar, why have I chosen to use *post*-modernism as a potential theoretical framework? The answer lies in the fact that, as I will focus on texts as the empirical ground for my analysis, I will need to refer to what Collins calls 'a

---

14 Huyssen quoted in Collins, 'Post-Modernism as Culmination', 95.

15 Collins, 'Post-Modernism as Culmination', 95–6.

Post-Modernist textual *practice*' as an important feature in the programmes under discussion. In particular, it is his identification of
'synchronicity' as a key feature within post-modernism and post-
modernist texts that is important.

> Modernist and Post-Modernist texts differ fundamentally . . . in
> their respective attitudes toward the 'already said'. The former
> constructs a dialogic relationship with previous representations
> only to reject them as outmoded, resulting in a semiotic zero-sum
> game. The latter constructs an entirely different relationship with
> the accumulated representational activity, recognising that this
> activity cannot be conjured away by a sudden rupture because it
> forms the very fabric of our 'structures of feeling'. Post-Modernist
> texts acknowledge that 'meaning', 'identity' etc., are complicated
> not only by the decentred nature of current political production,
> but also by the co-presence of previous representations persisting
> through the mass media—specifically television, which presents
> its own morphological continuity on a daily basis.[16]

As will become clear, the texts under discussion can not be con-
sidered 'avant-garde' or modernist in either their intent or form.
Instead, they demonstrate an acute sensitivity to the 'already said',
and resonate with a series of past references that are not only drawn
on retrospectively, but which are also understood to be coexistent,
or co-present. Collins and others also claim that such texts are
characteristically imbued with irony, playfulness, self-reflexivity, and
ambivalence. Post-modern texts embrace low or mass culture, and
juxtapose commercial culture with high art, thereby threatening
previous conceptions of authenticity, sincerity, and truth. All of these
aspects feature strongly in many of the programme texts I will be
analysing, as well as making links to characteristics and trends apparent within the 'baby-bust' generation under discussion.

This brings to light one further aspect of post-modernism that is
necessary to my arguments: the close association of post-modernism
with ambivalence. Ambivalence—the 'co-existence of two opposite
emotions'—will recur not only as a feature of the programmes, but
also as an attitude that young people have adopted more generally.
Generation X is ambivalent; not only in relation to television, but
within the wider context they are ambivalent because they find it
necessary or useful to be so. The usefulness of ambivalence is that it
can not be understood as an entirely negative, or defeatist attitude;
and in my discussion it will surface as an oscillation between, or even
the simultaneous presence of, both cynicism *and* enchantment.

16 Ibid., 108–9.

In a society over-burdened by the recurrent and pervasive presence of the 'already said' (and perhaps the 'already felt') within the media, as well as within social and private lifestyles, it is not surprising that young people felt cynical as they were obliged to buy into fashion, music, and behaviour patterns which appeared to be recycled. If such products and experiences had been validated somehow as part of a traditional 'rite of passage' this situation might not have been so awkward and its participants less cynical. Unfortunately, partly as a result of the mythologizing of youth culture in the 1960s, the only 'tradition' youth currently appears to be positively associated with is change, and perhaps, conflict—with older generations, with the state and/or society. Yet this tradition is based upon the existence of a unified and identifiable *status quo* which may then be challenged; in a post-modern culture, the '*status quo*' is difficult, if not impossible, to construct. In fact, an ambivalent incorporation into the fluctuating and chaotic processes of contemporary society may be the most appropriate, if not strictly the most subversive, tactic for such young people. A tacit incorporation that is armed by ambivalence would, after all, have the benefit of allowing many young people the possibility of enchantment; to suspend cynicism and to invest in the pleasures and practices available within the culture of commodities and virtual realities. It is an enchantment that will be necessarily contingent and perhaps temporary, and it offers experiences that may no longer be 'authentic' in a sense that might be comprehended by older generations; nevertheless, it is still an enchantment that fascinates and delights.

In the arguments which follow, there is an underlying tension. On the one hand, I will describe how the cynicism of many young people stems from a deep knowledge of the inauthenticity, the over-use, and the confusing over-abundance of different experiences, products, and practices within contemporary society—something that is both produced and reflexively encountered in many programmes addressed to youth. On the other hand, the continued exertions, tactics, and engagement of young people demonstrate the enchantment that binds them to that society—in programmes that also seduce, encourage, and absorb their young audience.

Having briefly sketched out the social and economic context for Generation X, it is now necessary to think through the issues and concerns that lie behind the co-option and address of youth by television. And I will suggest why, for a certain period, it became possible to perceive a mediated space in which the contradictory sensibility I have described was encouraged. Initially, this space was negotiated through the already existing conflict between the constructs 'television' and 'youth'.

Television   Television is perhaps the most ubiquitous of modern media technologies: available and used extensively in nearly all households in
Britain, it broadcasts to a potentially massive population of viewers.
The established structure of the television industry in Britain has
produced a situation in which a small number of production personnel commission, create, and transmit their programmes from a
relatively small number of locations. They broadcast their messages
to diffuse and diverse audiences, who still, predominantly, watch at
home. Whether the motivation has been one of public service or
arisen out of the need to create audiences for advertisers, larger
audiences are still deemed to prove the success of particular types of
programming. Historically, this has meant that both producers and
viewers have understood that much of what is produced for television
is defined by a series of ongoing compromises. For example, a compromise may result when producers are under pressure to address or
represent many different viewers, and thereby appeal to as large an
audience as possible. This may mean that producers find it more con-
venient to envisage such an audience through the construction of an
average viewer, who is, of course, no one in particular, nor existent in
reality. In response to this situation, a different kind of compromise
may also be reached by the viewer who, whilst knowing that he or
she is rarely *actually* addressed or represented by television, is nevertheless still willing to submit temporarily to a para-social discourse.
This discourse is conducted primarily through the direct address of
television to the viewer, and uses the inclusive 'you and me' of everyday social interaction; but it is in fact rarely, if ever, referring or
appealing to anybody in particular, or to any individual person at
all.[17] Television is therefore a media form which attempts to be inclusive; yet because of the compromises involved in such an endeavour
it is often believed to be guided by an appeal to the lowest common
denominator as it attempts to produce a culture that can be accessible
to all. In addressing nobody, television hopes to appeal to everybody.

Youth   In contrast to this, youth is a *part* of the wider population and has
long been understood in Britain as a distinct, significant, and active
segment of society, where individuals strive to present themselves as
somebody. Generations of youth are often seen by observers (and are
frequently articulated as such by young spokespeople themselves), as

17 See Donald Horton and R. Richard Wohl, 'Mass Communication and Para-Social
Interaction: Observations on Intimacy at a Distance', *Psychiatry*, 19 (1956), 215–23,
excerpted in John Corner and Jeremy Hawthorn (eds.), *Communication Studies: An
Introductory Reader* (4th edn., London: Edward Arnold, 1993), 156–65.

TABLE 1.1. *Youth and television: opposing constructs?*

YOUTH (*us*)	TELEVISION (*them*)
Alternative	Mainstream
Hip/cool	Straight/square/naff
Independent	Commercial
Authentic	False/phoney
Rebellious/radical	Conformist/conservative
Specialist genres	Pop
Insider knowledge	Easily accessible information
Minority	Majority
Heterogeneous	Homogeneous
Masculine culture	Feminine culture

being opposed to a dominant or mainstream culture (to, perhaps, 'everybody else'), which, more often than not, is identified with its presentation through the compromised medium of television. In Table 1.1, I have borrowed a table of categorizations that can be used to reveal how television and youth are naturally, and diametrically, opposed social and theoretical constructs.

Sarah Thornton constructed this table to delineate what she argues are the false dichotomies inherent in previous assessments of youth culture, with particular reference to numerous discussions concerning the distinctions between the 'us' of subcultures and the 'them' of mainstream culture.[18] My appropriation of some of her categorizations here is not intended to challenge her arguments but to point out how easily television could be substituted for her description of mainstream culture, and to observe how closely many conceptions of television fit with the terms provided here. So far, I have already indicated how television in Britain is produced under particular industrial or commercial pressures, which means that it has broadcast to the majority of the population in a way that, historically, has led to an imaginary construction of an homogeneous rather than a realistically heterogeneous audience. On top of this, television also offers 'easily accessible information', while the small screen's domestic context, along with the assumption that it is viewed passively, has meant that television as object and as cultural practice has often been feminized in both academic and popular discussions. And although television at specific moments may have produced specialized genres, its overarching discourse (its take on the wider culture) is ultimately 'pop'; generally acknowledged to be both superficial and

---

18 Adapted from Thornton, *Club Cultures*, 115.

determinedly populist. Value judgements, such as 'false/phoney', or 'straight/square/naff' and political associations such as 'conservative/conformist' may be more difficult to justify but they are all terms that have been attributed to television, particularly by young people. For example, as Thornton explains, a mainstream and 'symbolic' television show such as the BBC's *Top of the Pops* is clearly understood to be in opposition to the hip and radical aspirations of at least one aspect of youth culture today—the dance/rave scene. She explains:

> The show is considered so domestic, familial and accessible that the ultimate put-down is to say a club event was more '*Top of the Pops* than a warehouse rave' (*i-D* June 1990). Moreover, it is assumed that 'for dance music to stay vital, to mean more than the media crap we're fed from all angles, it has to keep *Top of the Pops* running scared' (*Mixmag* December 1991).[19]

While *Top of the Pops* does not represent all of television, the comments are representative of a common understanding of how television can and often does continue to function in opposition to the aspirations of youth and youth culture. Indeed, this opposition makes it possible to see how obviously television appears to be in conflict with the construction of youth identity, and how it may even be seen as contaminating in its attempts to approach or represent the supposedly authentic pleasures and activities of the young people themselves. Necessarily identified as 'other' to mainstream culture then, the study of youth and conceptions of youth culture have tended to be dominated by one of two perspectives emphasizing this alternative position. In a recent assessment of the state of play in youth studies, Thomas Ziehe usefully summarizes the situation and the conclusions which, inevitably, seem to be drawn from each approach:

> For some, youth tends to be a problem group in which symptoms of decadence are particularly pronounced; for others youth is the sole source of hope, whom we simply fail to understand properly.[20]

As Ziehe suggests, the study of youth has been traditionally located either within the study of deviance or within the younger discipline of cultural studies. Studies of deviant youth have examined moral panics, drug taking, and the problems of adolescence, and have unsurprisingly, therefore, tended to focus on youth as a 'symptom

---

19 Ibid., 123.

20 Thomas Ziehe, 'Cultural Modernity and Individualisation: Changed Symbolic Contexts for Young People', in Johan Fornas and Goran Bolin (eds.), *Moves in Modernity* (Stockholm: Almqvist & Wiskell, 1992), 73.

of decadence'.[21] Conversely, within cultural studies, the impetus is to describe and validate the culture of youth, often focusing on particular subcultures and their implications for the formation of identity. From this perspective, youth are often featured as creative, even expert, social semioticians, who play with, subvert, or resist the pressures of contemporary life. Youth is therefore celebrated as transcendent of, or as a locus for change within, the *status quo*. Thornton, in her summary of previous youth studies, notes how both approaches designate an 'other' against whom youth may be identified. She then goes on to point out that even the more progressive conceptions of youth —those generally, but not always, stemming from the left in political terms—implicitly construct this 'other' as gendered and lower class.

> On the one hand, youth are rebellious in their opposition to the mainstream as a complacent, dominant culture. On the other, the characteristics of the mainstream that they repeatedly disparage and subordinate in speech are those of the feminine working-class minority.[22]

Interestingly, these feminine and lower class (or low culture) characteristics are also—as I have suggested—often applied to television. Once more, this implies that there is an apparent contradiction in the attempt to wed the study of youth and television into a coherent whole. This is not to say that youth or young people do not watch or enjoy television—they clearly do—but it is also apparent, as Thornton states elsewhere in her book, that young people watch less television than other parts of the population. On top of this, when they do watch, they do so from a particularly cynical or suspicious perspective, particularly if and when they feel that television is attempting to represent or articulate their experience.

Ironically, even if it is accepted that youth do watch television (from whatever perspective), programmes directed at, or specifically produced for, youth are often the very programmes for which young people may reserve the most scorn. Indeed, even the most popular of the programmes I will discuss achieved relatively poor audience figures. For example, during my period of study (1987–95) it was a television import—the Australian soap *Neighbours* (on BBC1 since October 1986)—which gained the largest share of the young audience, and not the programmes specifically produced with them in mind.

Theoretically and socially, therefore, television and youth would seem to be very much at odds. In fact any attempt to address these constructs together might seem a little perverse. However, there is

---

21 A classic study that examines this phenomenon is Stanley Cohen, *Folk Devils and Moral Panics: The Creation of the Mods and Rockers* (London: MacGibbon and Kee, 1972).

22 Thornton, *Club Cultures*, 166.

one way in which, as theoretical constructs, 'youth' and 'television' have, rather unfortunately, much in common. This link has to do with how they are used by both popular and academic critics as presenting an opportunity for a holistic critique of the cultural *Zeitgeist*. Identifying this problem as it relates to the study of youth Thomas Ziehe describes the way in which some studies end up by apparently revealing a series of indicative cultural symptoms which have wide ramifications for Western society as a whole:

> In my experience another problem is that discussions of young people tend too quickly to adopt the form of the normatively overloaded diagnoses of the Zeitgeist. Such normative super elevation polarizes the theoretical subject of 'youth', giving it a firmly in-built evidential structure, with prosecutors and defendants.[23]

The ambitions evident in the kind of approach to which Ziehe is referring here are uncannily similar to many historical and current assessments of television's influence. In one recent example from Richard Dienst, there is clearly a suggestion that—almost by definition—the study of television must have far reaching implications for the understanding of Western culture and its future.

> In debates about globalization, cultural imperialism, dialectics of enlightenment, and so on, 'television' assumes a power beyond that attributed to its programming, as if its mere existence ensured certain effects, both ideological and physical. All of a sudden, at some point that should be within living memory, television seemed to flood the social sphere with a new kind of power.[24]

Television therefore seems—in some reports—to have a 'power beyond that attributed to its programming', in the same way that youth culture appears to have cultural influence beyond its real social or economic impact. In addition to this, it is possible to see that there are other associations to make, as revealed in the last part of Ziehe's statement. For if, as he states, youth studies is seen to be characterized by an 'in-built evidential structure, with prosecutors and defendants', this links the study of youth to television studies again. Television criticism—both popular and academic—has also been dominated by high-profile critics either for, or very much against, the pleasures and effects of the medium. The study of television and youth are alike, therefore, if only in that they are all too often riddled with critical or theoretical preoccupations that overdetermine how and why their subjects should be understood.

---

23 Ziehe, 'Cultural Modernity and Individualisation', 74.

24 Richard Dienst, *Still Life in Real Time: Theory after Television* (Durham, NC, and London: Duke University Press, 1994), 4.

While these possible pitfalls and obvious conflicts suggest that I should be very careful in linking youth to television, they have also begun to reveal how cynicism (though not yet enchantment) is inevitable in the relationship between youth and television. Yet it also makes it necessary to examine more closely why I wish to pursue this relationship and why I have chosen to look at youth television during this particular historical and social period.

The foundation of my study is pragmatic—in the short period 1987–95 it is possible to identify the rise and fall of a particular kind of youth programming in Britain. Different programmes worked together to construct an aesthetic practice and a cultural attitude that had implications both for the representation of youth and in the development of a wider television aesthetic. Other factors include the changes specific to the media environment, as well as certain identifiable characteristics (social and economic) that distinguish the particular generation of youth that were 'young' during this period. These changes and characteristics indicate that a different kind of relationship between youth and television, or, more loosely, youth and media technologies, was beginning to reveal itself. There was, I argue, a particular cultural moment where youth and television were consciously brought together in a way that revealed a great deal, both about television and the experience of viewing television.

British television in the late 1980s had gone through, and was to undergo, a variety of changes. Firstly, after 1982 there were four terrestrial channels, rather than three, with the new channel, Channel 4, obliged within its remit to cater for youth as a specific audience. On top of this, new satellite and cable channels became available over the course of the decade. The high profile launch of MTV Europe in 1987 had a significant impact, as it gained a prominent position in the emerging perception of a newly invigorated youth-directed media environment. MTV and other satellite and cable channels were also important for their crucial part in the changes taking place in the larger context of transnational media industries and technologies; these changes meant that television reached and defined its audience in a different way. For example, the shape of the electronic 'footprints' achieved geographically by satellite channels (that is, the area of the globe covered by a satellite and its range of channels) began, and continue, to organize the viewers who watch these channels into new and different kinds of community. Geographically and in terms of self-definition these communities are different, since by crossing national boundaries, and by targeting some parts of the population rather than others, such communities may be defined by links forged through taste and consumer power, as opposed to regional or national characteristics and their associated traditions. As David Morley and Kevin Robins suggest, the dissolving of such traditions has led to a series of contradictory pressures for the media involved. They argue that:

> the burden of catering to the various forms of 'nostalgia'—for a sense of community, tradition and belonging—falls increasingly on the electronic media at a time when they are, in fact, beginning to operate in new ways, often addressing geographically dispersed segments of different national or other communities.[25]

In the British context, for example, MTV was initially 'MTV Europe' and was obliged to negotiate the difficulties and contradictions inherent in the attempt to construct a European identity in opposition to the symbolic (and traditional) dominance of American or British youth culture. This attempt was obviously complicated by the presence of language differences and different life expectations on the part of its young audience.[26] Other writers are currently engaged in studying the processes and implications of this, and I will not attempt to cover this exhaustively in my own study, although I will return to certain aspects of MTV Europe in other chapters.[27] What I do want to remark on in this context, is how satellite channels and the emergence of other global media products—including videos, cassettes, as well as Walkmans, computer software, or pop stars—are associated with the emergence of other non-media global products such as fashion or food. New communities, based on taste and consumption patterns, rather than geography and nationality, as well as the global penetration of certain brands have led to the growth of markets-as-communities defined globally rather than nationally. Yet this does not necessarily imply homogeneity at a global level, as what emerges is in fact a process of intensification in the definition of a niche market (for goods, images, or music) which is then extended globally. This quote from Theodor Levitt's influential *The Marketing Imagination* demonstrates what this means in practice:

> Everywhere there is Chinese food, pitta bread, Country and Western music, pizza and jazz. The global pervasiveness of ethnic forms represents the cosmopolitanisation of speciality. Again, globalisation does not mean the end of segments. It means, instead, their expansion to worldwide proportions.[28]

25 David Morley and Kevin Robins, *Spaces of Identity: Global Media, Electronic Landscapes and Cultural Boundaries* (London: Routledge, 1995), 5.

26 Since the period in question, MTV Europe has fragmented into different national versions of MTV, with language differences and taste differentials—between northern and southern Europe—cited as the main reasons behind this shift.

27 See Lidia Hujic, 'I Hope You're Enjoying Your Party: MTV in Wartorn Bosnia', *Screen*, 37: 3 (Autumn 1996), 268–79.

28 Theodor Levitt, *The Marketing Imagination* (London: Collier-Macmillan, 1983), 30–1, quoted in Morley and Robins, *Spaces of Identity*, 113.

As a niche market defined by age and, to a certain extent, by taste, the effects of globalization have been taken up by, and exploited within, the still lucrative youth market to a degree that has begun to define the generation itself. In fact, some observers have gone as far as to identify the younger part of the 'baby-bust' generation as the 'global teen'. David Cannon explains:

> Invasive media has been used to promote brand names such as Benetton, Haagen Daaz, Nike, Esprit and Windows which are now part of the everyday language of *Generation X* around the planet. Described by some as the first global generation, they are joined together not by a common ideology but rather a sophisticated knowledge of consumer products.[29]

As Cannon goes on to elaborate, the young people of the late 1980s and 1990s—whether they are called 'baby-busters', 'global teens', or 'Generation X'—were not simply distinguished by their consumption of, or identification with, certain food and fashion products. Rather, their increasing use of, and familiarity with, different kinds of media underlined how this generation was now a participant within media networks, rather than simply passive recipients of media messages.

> This generation are the first to use computers as children. They are less technophobic as a consequence. Like foreign travel, technology has become increasingly accessible and even international. Telephone calls and fax machine use . . . are now part of the everyday life of young people. The proliferating use of the Internet of which teenagers are a surprisingly large user group, is again another transformational technology which is changing the nature of communication.[30]

In response to changing economic and demographic imperatives, terrestrial television in Britain in the late 1980s and 1990s was forced to adapt to a media environment that had changed in terms of technology, industry, and its audience. It did so in various ways, which necessarily affected the nature of terrestrial television in both content and form. Some of the most significant changes were inspired both by the new viewing habits of the audience and by the lowering of prices for certain media technologies. These came together in the way in which relatively lower prices and the erosion of the nuclear family encouraged a significant increase of sets per household in new locations such as the bedroom or kitchen. In Britain, the high penetration of video recorders (VCRs) meant that there was increased opportunity to view (both more programmes and at different times) as well as the

29 Cannon, 'Generation X', 2.

30 Ibid., 3.

possibility of watching pre-recorded videos. This increased opportunity for private viewing in different locations, as well as the potential for time-shifting, disrupted the traditional conception of families co-ordinating their viewing around a communal set at a particular time of day.

The response of terrestrial television to these changes was to extend and develop its schedules, reaching far into the night and into the early morning, covering almost twenty-four hours a day. There was also an increased attempt to respond to the fact that different audiences were now understood to watch at different times and for different reasons. One of the most high profile reactions of television companies caught up in the desire to capture these different audiences was the development of the 'morning show'—whether this was *This Morning* or the ill-fated *Good Morning* and *Vanessa*. All of these programmes attempted to reach and construct an audience of the unemployed, students, housewives, and the elderly who would be available to view at this time of day. The youth audience, however, proved particularly difficult to pin down. Initially, programmes aimed at this audience were scheduled in early evening slots (6–7.30 p.m.) only to be confined later to night time viewing (10 p.m.–3.30 a.m.).

Aside from the issue of its scheduling, youth television was also sensitive to the new media environment and to the new horizons of its target audience in the determination of its content. While many youth programmes covered familiar youth culture territory such as fashion and music, other programmes attempted to address the broader horizons of the global teen—most obviously, in a travel programme such as the *Rough Guide To . . .* series. Other programmes explicitly acknowledged their target audience's greater familiarity with computer technology, in programmes such as *Gamesmaster*, but also in shows such as *The Crystal Maze*. A greater mix of media and genre was also evident in this generation of youth programmes; whether it was in adult animation, in *Liquid TV* and *Beavis and Butthead* (on MTV and Channel 4) and *The Simpsons* (on Sky/BBC) or through the use of new technologies to produce programmes. In particular, the camcorder emerged as a familiar tool and was used in both the *Teenage Diaries* and in *Takeover TV*. Even in the well-honed area of music programming, terrestrial television made some attempt to reflect the global/niche aspects of taste distinctions present in different parts of the youth audience. Whilst minority programmes with a global reach were introduced, such as the 'indie' music show *Snub TV*, simultaneously there was an increasing enthusiasm for programmes in which the global identity of youth might be represented. Several music-culture magazine programmes—*Rapido* and *Passengers* —either attempted to unify youth across the globe, or simply celebrated the cultural diversity of youth within Europe and over the planet.

In their aesthetic values many of the programmes also developed strategies that sprang from a wish to attract an audience that programme makers believed was no longer watching television in the same way as previous generations. By the mid-1980s and 1990s youth were an audience potentially distracted by the proliferation of other media; a suspicion encouraged by the publishing boom in the 1980s, enabling this generation far greater access to a range of magazines specifically aimed at them. A simultaneous 'freeing' of the airwaves also meant that young people had an increasing choice of, and greater opportunity to listen to, new radio stations, in addition to the much vaunted threat of computer games.

This television audience was also more comfortable with the concept, and with the use, of television as a multi-purpose *screen* rather than as a television *set*. In the new viewing environments, the television screen could represent nothing more than moving wallpaper, or be used for computer games or videos instead. This meant that the small screen was no longer exclusively reserved for television. For this generation, unlike previous generations, television had always been *there*; they did not grow up with television, it was already an old domestic machine, and its content far from special. It is not surprising that the strategies employed by many of the programmes aimed at this generation of youth were designed to negotiate the mundane and everyday qualities of the television medium itself.

Ironically, these strategies can be seen to have been organized through a reworking of the *televisual* aspects of television. These aspects—relating primarily to the nature of the image and the appearance of immediacy and spontaneity—were continually emphasized in youth programmes, restating perversely what was peculiar to television in opposition to film or other media. It is therefore these televisual aspects—the construction of liveness and spontaneity, and the aesthetics of the image—that I will focus on in the chapters which follow.

Generation X emerged as an identifiable part of the population who could be recognized not simply by their age—which could be anything from 15–34—but more precisely by their consumption patterns or, as I will discuss in the next chapter, more intuitively, through their 'attitude'. What is particularly interesting, however, is the self-consciousness of their construction as a commodity in their own right. Simon Frith, in his article 'Youth/Music/Television' explains the factors behind television's attempt to attract this audience in the late 1980s and early 1990s.

the 'youth' audience was a valuable commodity, in demand by British advertisers, and British television companies began, for the first time, to do systematic market research, to check programmes (like *The Bill* and even *Coronation Street*) for youth appeal.[31]

This generation of viewers can be understood, therefore, to be an actual population of possible television viewers whose interests and pleasures were putatively addressed by the rash of youth programmes produced from the late 1980s on. Unfortunately, the final equation between the programmes under consideration and the young people in question is not really so straightforward. Firstly, many of the programmes were produced by the BBC—supposedly immune to commercial incentives and directed more explicitly by its public service commitment. Secondly, it could be argued that what was also occurring during the period in question—when perhaps, 'youth programming' became 'yoof TV'—was that the audience (the *actual* young people) began to disappear. Indeed, many of the original young viewers (obviously) got older and were no longer young or youthful. Yet in terms of genre, various programmes continued to have presenters and production personnel in common; they thus had coincidences of form, content, and appeal which were not necessarily tied to an intent to attract a specific youth audience. The form and content of youth programming in this period therefore became detached from its original audience and developed as an aesthetic that would be adapted by many other television programmes. As two articles in the *Guardian* newspaper suggested, the impact of 'yoof' programmes had a significant effect on British television in general, with ramifications for a far wider audience than those people who were young or youthful during the late 1980s and early 1990s. Stephen Armstrong, commemorating the inception of the original late 1980s youth programme, *Network 7*, writes:

> It spawned the word 'yoof', it gave us *The Big Breakfast* and
> Janet Street-Porter, it made Sunday lunchtime television
> watchable for the first time since *Thunderbirds* . . . From an idea
> by Janet Street-Porter and Jane Hewland at LWT, the programme
> was commissioned by John Cummins, head of youth at Channel
> 4, made two series, won a BAFTA award and slipped away into
> TV history. Since then, almost everyone associated with the
> programme has gone on to shape British television—whether
> as director-general of the BBC (John Birt was director of
> programmes at LWT and called the show 'an inspiration') or
> maverick TV whiz-kid (the feuding twins of funky TV, Charlie
> Parsons and Sebastian Scott both worked on the programme).[32]

31 Simon Frith, 'Youth/Music/Television', in Simon Frith, Andrew Goodwin, and Larry Grossberg (eds.), *Sound & Vision: The Music Video Reader* (London: Routledge, 1993), 73.

32 Stephen Armstrong, 'Yoof's Rebel Rousers', *Guardian*, 12 May 1997, 8–9 (media supplement).

Yet it was not only the production personnel who were to become influential; Michael Bracewell summarizes a sensibility that has clear links with the form and content of many of the youth programmes I will discuss. In a discussion centring on contemporary entertainment programmes—including *Live and Kicking, Shooting Stars*, and *Never Mind the Buzzcocks*—he suggests that:

> These programmes can be seen to represent a particular attitude within popular media, in which self-parody and self-reference, *ad infinitum*, is the driving force. The accent is on bogus sincerity and the collectively raised eyebrow, sending up the whole idea that anyone, including the presenters and the production staff, could actually be taking this stuff seriously. As an exercise in wholesale regression, these shows are informed by the kindergarten wackiness of *Tiswas* and *OTT*, which date from the adolescence or early adulthood, in the late seventies and early eighties, of today's new generation of presenters.[33]

How or why did this happen? The answer lies in the slippery and fragile definition of youth and its increasing detachment from the real or actual audience. Simon Frith explains:

> one way of reading the problem of youth TV in the late 1980s is as an attempt to develop a sharper lifestyle account of youth, to devise a form of youth programming that could float quite free of any structural base. In this model 'youth' became a category constructed by TV itself, with no other referent: those people of whatever age or circumstance who watched 'youth' programmes became youth, became, that is, *the future of television*.[34]

Thus the period my study covers (1987–95) will embrace another contradiction: while it is clearly a period when a real generation of young people could be identified, and were addressed by the various programmes made explicitly to attract them, there is also a sense in which the aesthetic that these programmes generated became increasingly detached from its original audience and emerged, as Frith suggests, as 'the future of television'. The conclusion to this development is made clear by the recent (1996) dropping of the word 'Youth' from the title of the department previously known as 'Youth and Entertainment' at the BBC. Whilst one understanding of this might be that youth as an audience was being abandoned, it is clear that the youthful attitude developed by 'yoof TV' has not. Recent successes such as the quiz shows *Shooting Stars* and *They Think It's All Over* share a reliance on a balance of cynicism and enchantment, and

33 Michael Bracewell, 'The Clone Zone', *Guardian*, 7 Apr. 1997, 2–3 (media supplement).
34 Frith, 'Youth/Music/Television', 75.

both are produced by independent companies (Channel X and Talkback respectively) responsible for previous youth programmes. 'Yoof', therefore, as Bracewell laments, is now clearly part of, rather than necessarily distinct from, entertainment—at least as far as the BBC is concerned. While the renaming of the department reveals the changing imperatives, and contemporary adjustments to the structure and expressed ambitions of the BBC more generally, it also demonstrates how the shift from youth to yoof programmes during this period is a response to the way in which the television audience (as a whole) was seen to be changing. More than simply responding to the need to address or represent a particular group of individuals, yoof television articulated the pressures of a television industry that was adjusting to an upheaval in its internal structure, and to an apparent loss of purchase on its audience.

This distinction, or separation between audience and aesthetic, reveals an uncanny doubling of the youth that is at the heart of my enquiry. While there was a real generation of young people who were the inspiration for a particular kind of television programming, it will be increasingly evident that what I am actually describing is a viewing sensibility which responds to the aesthetic these programmes developed. As Frith notes, this is a viewing sensibility which is not necessarily only adopted or understood by this specific generation of young people. It is better understood as a sensibility that is primarily informed by an experience of television, or an accumulation of knowledge about television, which cannot be confined solely to this particular generation of television viewers.

The shifts between audience and aesthetic which occur throughout the book are related to the shifts within the television industry itself during this particular period of time. However, my examination of yoof television also gives me an opportunity to make some comments about the nature of television viewing more generally. This critical space is generated by one further element informing my work. Many of my observations are based on my personal interpretation. While this is an interpretation that is informed by my experience as a regular television viewer it is also, during the period in question, the experience of a *youthful* television viewer. As I write, I am also doubled; while I am (not coincidentally) at times a member of the audience I describe, I am also an ageing observer whose views are partial and emotional. For anthropologists this has long been a necessary and complex problematic, but for a media analyst it has perhaps only recently been recognized as something that is not simply a quandary, but an opportunity. In an article in *Screen* Annette Kuhn identifies a similar problem/opportunity as she discusses her own relationship to a media text, the British 'social problem' film *Mandy* (1952):

Emotion and memory bring into play a category with which film theory—and cultural theory more generally—are ill equipped to deal: experience. Indeed they have been wary even of making any attempt to deal with it, often rightly so. For experience is not infrequently played as the trump card of authenticity, the last word of personal truth; forestalling all further discussion, let alone analysis. Nevertheless, experience is undeniably a key category of everyday knowledge, structuring people's lives in important ways . . . —my memories, my feelings—are important because these things make me what I am, make me different from everyone else. Must they be consigned to a compartment separate from the part of me that thinks and analyses? Can the idea of experience not be taken on board—if with a degree of caution— by cultural theory, rather than being simply evaded or, worse, assigned to the realm of sentimentality and nostalgia?[35]

Kuhn is writing from her own particular—and highly regarded— position within the discipline of film studies, and my ambitions are more narrowly focused than hers. Yet, unlike Kuhn, I am supported by television studies' recent embrace of a broadly phenomenological approach to the process of viewing, as well as its traditionally less rigorous adherence to any governing theoretical doctrine.[36]

Nevertheless, several features of Kuhn's and my own approach necessarily coincide. Memory, emotion, and experience inform many of the observations that follow and their incorporation has been vital in my attempt to map out a specific television aesthetic. The acknowledgement of my own relationship to television should demonstrate that the *experience* of television—which involves both memories of television, and memories *informed* by television, as well as the emotions television generates—are factors that need to be revalued in the attempt to understand how television works.

35 Annette Kuhn, '*Mandy* and Possibility', *Screen*, 33: 3 (Autumn 1992), 237.

36 Some of my arguments here are akin to those outlined in Paddy Scannell, *Radio, Television and Modern Life: A Phenomenological Approach* (Oxford: Blackwell, 1996).

2

Network 7
Youth becomes 'Yoof'

TELEVISION has a spatial dimension that has often been under-
estimated; less awe inspiring than the space imbued with fantasy
and desire that exists between the spectator and the big screen
in the cinema, the space television produces is more encroaching
and more flexible. As the television viewer dozes, grooms, chats, eats,
moves closer or further away from the small screen, turns the sound
up or down, changes channels or checks the schedule via teletext, this
space is stretched, squashed, ignored, or distorted. While it is true
that, on occasions, television offers something similar to the place
organized by the cinema—where spectators sit silently before the
screen giving it their full attention—much of the time the place constructed by television is clearly less static than this. Doreen Massey's
useful observations concerning the articulation of space in contemporary life make it possible to understand what kinds of affective
place television produces for each viewer. Using her observations as a
point of departure, the television experience, rather than being like
(or a poor imitation of) cinema, can be seen to function in a very
different manner. The durational, habitual aspects of television viewing mean that it produces something akin to the kind of affective
topography Massey describes below, as she takes the reader for a walk
through her neighbourhood in Kilburn, north London:

> Thread your way through the often almost stationary traffic
> diagonally across the road from the news-stand and there's a
> shop which as long as I can remember has displayed saris in the
> window. Four life-sized models of Indian women, and reams of
> cloth. On the door a notice announces a forthcoming concert at
> Wembley Arena: 'Anand Miland presents Rekha', another ad for
> the end of the month is written, 'All Hindus are cordially invited'.
> In another newsagents I chat with the man who keeps it, a Muslim
> unutterably depressed by events in the Gulf, silently chafing at
> having to sell *The Sun*. Overhead there is at least one aeroplane
> —we seem to be on a flight path to Heathrow and by the time
> they're over Kilburn you can see them clearly enough to tell the

airline and wonder as you struggle with your shopping where they're coming from.[1]

Massey's experience enables her to argue that places can not be understood as static, concrete territories:

> Instead then, of thinking of places as areas with boundaries around, they can be imagined as articulated moments in networks of social relations and understandings, but where a large proportion of those relations and understandings are constructed on a far larger scale than what we happen to define for that moment as the place itself, whether that be a street, or a region or even a continent.[2]

What she demonstrates is that each and any place can be understood as a vibrant situation that is almost humming with the connections it forms and reforms with places and spaces elsewhere. Television, I argue, constantly strives to reproduce this kind of experience. Whilst watching television, as much as walking down their local high street, individuals unconsciously oscillate between local knowledges and the potential of any place as an 'articulated moment' in 'networks of social relations and understandings', in other words, the connections or reach that the most mundane of local places has to the global—to both real and imagined sites, memories and dreams. Television, then, is local and global in this unconscious sense, not just in news reports or documentaries, but in its graphic interludes and via the television presenter's mode of address. In fact much of television exists simply to direct and coax the viewer to move between different kinds of place and space.[3]

Massey's journey is therefore a useful way to think about the activity of television viewing. In the process of viewing, young people and other audiences also take this kind of familiar path; they too negotiate, cross over, and shift between different meanings produced by different kinds of place. The way in which young people, as opposed to other audience members, watch television, and the choices they make—more or less deliberately—are influenced by their needs, biographies, and fantasies. For, as Massey suggests:

> People's route through the place, their favourite haunts within it, the connections they make (physically, or by phone or post, or in

1 Doreen Massey, *Space, Place and Gender* (Cambridge: Polity Press, 1994), 153.

2 Ibid., 154.

3 See, for example, Margaret Morse, 'Television Graphics and the Virtual Body: Words on the Move', in Margaret Morse, *Virtualities: Television, Media Art and Cyberculture* (Bloomington, Ind.: Indiana University Press, 1998), 71–99. And John T. Caldwell, 'Franchiser: Digital Packaging/Industrial Strength Semiotics', in John T. Caldwell, *Televisuality: Style, Crisis and Authority in American Television* (New Brunswick, NJ: Rutgers University Press, 1995), 134–60.

memory and imagination) between here and the rest of the world vary enormously.[4]

Young people take different routes—watch different programmes in different places at different times and in different ways—from other viewers. How and why they do this will differ again, but, as I will demonstrate, television attempts to direct these viewers through a series of identifiable generic and aesthetic strategies.

Newly established as commissioning editor for youth programmes, Stephen Garrett was asked about the audience for his programmes. His response was, perhaps, surprising:

> The wonderful thing about being Commissioning Editor for Youth Programming is that there's no such thing as youth programming. I don't have this vision of a spotty 19-year old in Nottingham to whom I'm saying. 'This is a programme for you!'[5]

Surprising, since in Britain, from the demise of the toddler's truce in 1957,[6] there have been—in contrast to this disclaimer—many British television programmes specifically designed with a particular kind of young viewer in mind. Whilst the earliest of these shows—such as the *Six-Five Special*, *Oh Boy!*, and *Ready, Steady, Go*—were predominantly music based, later shows such as *The Oxford Road Show* and *Something Else* also attempted to address other issues, such as politics, fashion, sexuality, and the arts—as and when they could be made relevant to the young viewer. In the 1970s and 1980s, other light entertainment programmes such as *The Multi-Coloured Swap-Shop* and *Tiswas*, whilst not necessarily targeting the youth audience—being primarily aimed at children—were also successful in attracting a teenage following.

What Garrett's flippant comments reveal instead is that, as a commissioning editor addressing Generation X, he was very careful not to label a particular individual or even a group of individuals as representative of contemporary youth. The increasing fragmentation of the youth audience and expanding diversity of different media that I outlined in the previous chapter obliged programme makers to be

---

4 Massey, *Space, Place and Gender*, 153.

5 Quoted in Simon Frith, 'Youth/Music/Television', in Simon Frith *et al.* (eds.), *Sound & Vision: The Music Video Reader* (London: Routledge, 1993), 69.

6 The 'toddlers truce' was an hour between 6 and 7 p.m. when television went off air; its existence was meant to enable parents to get their recalcitrant children to bed. Various industry and commercial pressures, most prominently the recently launched ITV television companies (ITV went on air in 1955), encouraged the Postmaster-General (then responsible for broadcasting) no longer to demand this. One of the first programmes to prove a success in this new slot was the BBC's *Six-Five Special* which was aimed at the new teenage, 'rock'n'roll' market. For more on this in relation to youth programming see John Hill, 'Television and Pop: The Case of the 1950s', in John Corner (ed.), *Popular Television in Britain* (London: British Film Institute, 1991), 90–107.

wary of trying to homogenize or unify this audience too explicitly. The producers' strategy in targeting this diverse population was to align themselves with contemporary style magazines aimed at the youth market. In the 1980s, new publications such as *Sky*, *The Face*, and *i-D* had, in sharp contrast to the traditionally narrow focus of the older youth publications, defined a lifestyle or attitude to the world, and expanded their horizons to incorporate fashion, drugs, television, and film as well as music.[7] Their take on popular culture was irreverent and flirtatious—the ever present 'wink' on the cover of *i-D*, for example, made this clear.[8] While this youthful attitude, or style, was never satisfactorily defined—by its very nature it could not or should not have been—in relation to television one dominant assumption was that it implied an audience 'who probably haven't got a lot of responsibilities'. Janet Street-Porter, the original editor of Youth and Entertainment at the BBC is reported as saying:

> I'd like to be called head of 'different' programmes or 'youth*ful*' programmes . . . I suppose the programmes we make are for people who don't have a lot of responsibilities. The minute you have a *lot* of responsibilities, you stop being receptive to new ideas. As soon as you have a really big mortgage or maybe a baby, you probably don't have as much money left to go out and buy records, or perhaps you can't go to clubs as easily, or you go to the cinema less frequently. That's not to say your brain dies, it just gets harder to do a lot of things. So if I was to specify the people that I think watch the programmes, I'd have to say they're people who probably haven't got a lot of responsibilities![9]

How this attitude might actually be reflected in the programmes themselves was suggested by Bill Hilary, interviewed shortly after he was appointed as commissioning editor for youth programmes at Channel 4 (at one time he had also been deputy to Janet Street-Porter). Hilary claimed that he:

> also believes there is still a viewing market defined less by age than by 'attitude', that wants 'television that is fresh and not afraid to ask questions, programmes that are slightly wild and different and unafraid to stand against the status quo'.[10]

7 By this I mean British weekly newspapers, popularly known as the 'inkies' such as *Melody Maker* and the *NME* which focused on music, and, in this period, indie or rock music, almost exclusively.

8 Every cover star for the magazine is captured winking at the camera—a gesture that is jokey, flirtatious, and about 'being looked at', a combination that resonates very much with the character of Generation X. It also suggests collusion; a knowing intimacy.

9 Janet Street-Porter quoted in Simon Frith, 'Youth/Music/Television', 75.

10 Bill Hilary quoted in Lisa O'Kelly, 'Youngsters Just Wanna Have Fun', *Independent*, 22 July 1992, 15.

While his comments demonstrate an appeal to the broadly public service requirements within Channel 4's remit—that it 'answer needs not met elsewhere in the broadcasting system' and 'innovate and experiment in form as well as content'—Hilary, like Street-Porter, understands this youth audience as being primarily defined through their 'attitude' to the world. Thus youth is not a group of individuals defined by age, but an audience who share tastes and ambitions. In his version, they are not just 'without responsibilities' but want 'fresh television' that is 'slightly wild'. They are therefore—implicitly—tired of conventional television.

Network 7 was the first programme that demonstrated the attitude Street-Porter and Hilary were so keen to advocate. Originally edited by Janet Street-Porter before she went to act as Youth Editor for the BBC, *Network 7*'s importance to youth television is not only because many of its personnel (both on and off screen) would go on to work on other youth-oriented shows, but because it can be identified as the instigator of many televisual characteristics that were to become endemic in later youth programmes.[11] Indeed, as previously noted, it has been identified as the programme where youth was to become 'yoof'.[12] In terms of its format the programme was much like other magazine shows past and present—it combined a mix of serious and lighter items, and integrated in-studio interviews with location reports and videotape inserts. Its distinctiveness lay in its exclusive appeal to the youth audience and its amateurish style of presentation. Wobbly cameras, long tracking shots, fluffing presenters, garish graphics dominating the screen, frequent continuity blunders and a general air of chaos made the show feel and look different.

The disorientation of the camera's swoops and odd angles was supplemented by the fact that the presenters were never given a secure position in the studio from which to anchor themselves. Many items were linked from what appeared to be a dressing room or trailer, or, alternatively, the presenters were on the move, awkwardly traipsing across acres of cable-strewn floor. The programme had abandoned the desks, sofas, and fixed 'three camera set up' of the traditional magazine programme—such as the BBC's *Breakfast Time*—and exposed the television studio for what it was: an open, chaotic space.

---

11 Presenters included Sankha Guha who went on to present the 'youth' travel programme *Rough Guide to the* . . . as well as Sebastian Scott, who, with Charlie Parsons (who also worked on the show) went on to produce programmes such as *The Big Breakfast* and *The Word*.

12 'Yoof' was used as a way of describing many of the programmes I will discuss. What it actually infers is not exactly clear; obviously 'yoof' indicates a kind of cockneyed (and therefore working-class) version of youth, indicating the sort of pose that might be taken up by those aspiring to be 'street wise'. It is also likely that it was coined to parody Janet Street-Porter's own notoriously strangled London accent, well known from her own history as a television presenter.

While the anonymous white walls and floor of the studio remained constant, guests, presenters, bands, and other cabaret acts were scattered about seemingly at random. The disruption of the traditional order of the television studio, and the refusal to create an illusion of a real place—a living room or news room—created an atmosphere of unpredictability and ambivalence. In one programme, one item concerned a group of young people 'coming out' to their friends and family. Simultaneously, elsewhere in the studio, another item involved members of the crew building a temple in which a guest attempted to 'channel' to extra-terrestrials on the other side of the galaxy. Neither item demanded that the viewer take it seriously. The channelling temple, unsurprisingly, was a spoof, and the earnest guest was made to look ridiculous surrounded by bamboo chairs and pot plants. Yet, unintentionally perhaps, the 'coming out' of the different young people was also ambivalently presented, since the participants were awkwardly clumped together without proper chairs or a stage to speak from. This meant that the different confessions and the reactions of friends and family became muddled and unfocused.

At a surface level this muddle was also exacerbated by the use of graphics and subtitles which often blocked out elements of the screen, or scrolled across the bottom of the shot. Whilst sometimes simply giving the title to a particular item, at other points the graphics provided extra information—statistics, comments, or jokes—which, placed over the image, often obscured the presenter as he or she spoke directly to camera. The level of visual 'noise' was therefore higher than previous magazine programmes, and this 'overloading' was to become a trademark of the yoof style.[13] In Street-Porter's later show *Rough Guide to . . .* the use of graphics and other visual excesses were again very much in evidence, much to the irritation of some critics:

> What I don't like about *Rough Guide* is what it has in common with every other Young People show. There's a loathing of cameras held steadily enough for you to see anything, an obsession with splitting the screen into six bits and showing the same picture in all of them, and an endless stream of subtitles telling you eight things while De Vine and/or Guha are telling you five more— which usually means you remember absolutely nothing at all.[14]

13 Particularly busy shows included *Reportage*, a news magazine show, the music show *Dance Energy*—both edited by Street-Porter for her Def II strand—and the Def II identity itself, which relied on highly stylized graphic interludes and titles to 'separate' its schedule from the other programmes surrounding it on BBC2. Even more mainstream shows such as *The Chartshow* (on ITV) were 'busy', in this instance the programme mimicked Apple Mac computer graphics on top of the visual image to provide information and comment about the music videos being shown. In a slightly more contained manner, later shows such as *The Big Breakfast* and *TFI Friday* also use graphics and graphic interludes in an excessive manner.

14 Patrick Stoddart, 'A Rough Guide to the Streetwise', *Observer*, 17 Aug. 1988, 20.

Yet a busy screen, layered with information, might not be irritating for younger viewers, if they were, as programme makers suspected, watching distractedly and engaging with the programme sporadically. Instead, a busy, information-heavy image could be useful if the target audience were watching with the sound turned down. This youth audience might easily watch television, do their homework, have phone conversations, or listen to their own music all at the same time. In relation to Generation X, the busy screen and information overload implied (even if it did not necessarily mean) that they, as an audience, were self-consciously media literate.

The programme's resonance for younger viewers also related to their living environment; many young people live and create places that are busy, messy, and muddled. For the young person, their bedroom—where walls, mirrors, and windows might be decorated with stickers, posters, graffiti, trophies, postcards, and ticket stubs— is a familiar and often chaotically busy site/sight. Here, different kinds of visual, and written, material—photographs, badges, and schedules —harbour a series of different meanings. In this way, favourite rock bands, football clubs, relationships, parties, holidays, and information about school or college are seemingly placed at random, often making little sense to the older observer. The busyness of *Network 7* is similar to this kind of environment; interests, persons, events are scattered within the studio and over the screen in the same way as the bedroom develops as a palimpsest of the young person's public and private self.

Like the decor in the bedroom, the items in *Network 7* are easily dismissed or substituted. The transience of stars and events on the show are like the suddenly un-hip pop star who is quickly relegated to the dustbin or younger siblings' rooms. Thus the programme's presentation of popular culture, like the bedroom, may make sense only to the inhabitant who actually lives there. Rather than presenting a coherent biographical narrative, which would need to acknowledge the existence of a history, the programme, like the self-conscious teenager's bedroom, presents a fragmented vision of current likes and fantasies and quickly dismisses or covers over the past. The programme's usefulness, and meaningfulness to the young person, lies in its ability to address this 'present-ness' of everyday experience, and the increasingly frenetic pace and turnover of what is desirable and cool within the worlds of film, television, fashion, and music. In its frantic pace the programme replicates each young person's negotiation and varied attempts to participate in a popular culture that attempts to possess them, and which is important, both in relation to how others see them, and how they wish to present themselves.

Generation X, like other youth generations, valued the right kind of knowledge about the right kind of subjects: popular culture, commodities, labels, and brands. What was different was that, increasingly, in the late 1980s and 1990s, knowledge as knowledge—'knowing' in both senses of the word—became valuable in its own right:

> Common to all the younger people in our study was a delight in collecting bits of information, facts, jargon and trivia. In their personal lives this might translate into a sophisticated knowledge of music or mountain bikes . . . Special knowledges are constantly traded among young people and represent a kind of status symbol to those who possess them. Monitored conversations between young people from school leavers to Oxford firsts show less emphasis on the sharing of thoughts and feelings, and more on exchanging information about consumer products and services which they know a great deal about.[15]

Network 7 therefore presented—without claiming any particular authority—a grab bag of information, facts, and trivia that could be exchanged and traded, whether or not viewers actually went to see the films, places, and rock bands or really understood the different issues and beliefs presented on screen. In this *Network 7* was again like the style magazines that were clearly the inspiration for the programme in the first place. The programme's visual style, too, had also borrowed heavily from these different publications. Every week in *Smash Hits*, every month in *The Face* and *i-D*, images were overlaid with print, paragraphs stretched and pushed around, typeface distorted, coloured, and fragmented. Readers of these magazines were unlikely to be overwhelmed by a busy screen 'telling you eight things while [the presenters] are telling you five more'. In any event, young people were already familiar with the business of 'reading around' images and print. Comics many would have read in childhood used the space on the page imaginatively, and encouraged a different and more playful approach to reading print and image. In the late 1980s and early 1990s this approach was further validated or recalled by the way in which comics 'grew up'. The success of adult comics such as the smutty *Viz*, the trend-setting nature of smaller publications such as *Deadline*, as well as the brief mainstream success of the 'graphic novel', all relied on this different form of reading.[16] Reading around

---

15 David Cannon, 'Generation X and the New Work Ethic', a Demos working paper (London: Demos, 1994), 7–8.

16 *Deadline* was the first to publish Jamie Hewlitt's 'Tank Girl' series which gained enough of a fan base to be developed into an ill-fated film of the same name. This dismal fate was not met by the graphic novel series *The Dark Knight*. This novel was the basis for the mainstream success of Tim Burton's first *Batman* (1989) film. The novel's retelling of the Batman story, presenting the hero as a much more complex and ambivalent figure than before, was adopted by Burton, as was the novel's excessive gothic and grotesque aesthetic.

the image was not distracting or irritating to younger viewers, it was familiar and increasingly fashionable.

Yet being fashionable or cool could not be determined solely by the surface aspect of the programmes. As the yoof style developed, the attitude that Street-Porter and Hilary had alluded to was increasingly articulated through a form of presentation, borrowed from radio, known as 'Zoo':

> Essentially, Zoo, on radio or TV, means that you can hear the people making the show sniggering in the background. That's only the starting point. Zoo also involves improvisation, irreverence, in-jokes, deep trivia and disposable news. It's also a clever conjuring trick. It's a way of going live and not going belly-up—mistakes are part of the fun.[17]

Whilst the mistakes in *Network 7* had never been apologized for—indeed they were a guarantee of the programme's spontaneity and authenticity—in Zoo TV this characteristic became excessive and mistakes became an essential element. Programmes produced after *Network 7*, such as *The Word*, *The Big Breakfast*, and *MTV's Most Wanted*, as well as more recent programmes like *Don't Forget Your Toothbrush I & II* and *TFI Friday*, all borrowed and exaggerated the Zoo aesthetic. All these programmes, in different ways, used in-jokes, self-reflexivity, parody, and often simply bad taste, to break down the seamlessness of television and its *status quo*.

Importantly, the *status quo* under attack was not within wider society; rather it was a rebellion against the televisual *status quo*, and conventional television. As such, the programmes were also always *about* television, and this audience's familiarity with its illusions:

> Zoo TV, when it works, takes away any pretence or mystique . . . It's a little less patronising to the viewers. Everybody knows how TV is made. We've grown up with it. We've got camcorders. People know there are actually 25 people standing in the room watching, so why should we pretend that there's just the two presenters cosily sat on a sofa simulating a suburban relationship?[18]

Network 7 pre-empted the Zoo style on television in that it created a place that was deliberately chaotic. One of the most striking things about the show was in its use of hand-held cameras or cameras that were otherwise particularly mobile. In terms of conventional tele-visual grammar, a mobile, clumsy camera style creates a 'lively' feel and accelerates the pace of the programme. In addition, due to its

---

17 Jim McLellan, 'Down the Tube', *The Face*, 54 (Mar. 1993), 50.

18 Sebastian Scott quoted in McLellan, 'Down the Tube', 52–3.

associations with the 'fly-on-the-wall' documentary genre, it is seen to guarantee intimacy, honesty, and legitimate voyeurism. While both these elements were important to the show, the mobile camera also placed the programme in an apparently contradictory position. While the presence of such an obvious camera technique revealed that the programme makers felt that the 'look' of the programme *was* important, the amateurish nature of this technique implied that they couldn't care less. Implicitly, *Network 7*'s lack of production values was related to a disregard for conventional television practices, and thus for television itself. Wobbly cameras produced an exciting visual image, but they also implied, at least to viewers who were comfortable with technologies such as the camcorder, that they could have done this too—if they had wanted. They might even have done it better. This suggested that *Network 7* was a television programme that was made by people who were like their audience, and who were, therefore, not simply anonymous and potentially patronizing television professionals.

In later yoof programmes the mobility of the camera developed to the extent that it appeared to have a personality of its own. In these shows the camera lens was no longer transparent, and had abandoned the pretence that the television camera was a metaphorical, all seeing eye.[19] In the MTV Europe programme, *MTV's Most Wanted*, the camera zoomed, panned, and shook in reaction to the presenter's—Ray Cokes's—questions and suggestions. In this way, Ray and the camera appeared to engage in a form of choreographed banter. This could either draw the viewers in, as they identified with the camera's persona, or alienate them, for by being constantly reminded of the mediation of the television image—the presence of the camera lens—their supposedly untrammelled relationship with Ray was being disrupted.

Such disruption by technology or by other anthropomorphic pals was not exactly new. This style of presentation has its antecedents in the long tradition of presenters and puppet sidekicks on British television, going back as far as Basil Brush and Muffin the Mule. In these instances the puppet co-host acts as a foil to the presenter's discourse. Interestingly, there were several successful puppet/presenter partnerships on screen at the same time as many of the youth programmes I am discussing. Aside from the children's continuity announcers and their puppet pals—Philip Schofield and Gordon the Gopher, or more recently, Otis the Aardvark with a variety of presenters—Chris

---

19 This more aggressive pose might be seen to have been championed by MTV, particularly as in one recurring visual ident MTV claimed to be 'In Your Eye'. This suggests that rather than gazing or glancing at the screen, the MTV viewer might experience television as if it were 'a poke in the eye', and therefore be provoked, rather than passively entertained.

Evans was cavorting with the puppet aliens, Zig and Zag, on *The Big Breakfast*. What was different—and perhaps *The Big Breakfast* is the best example of this—is that in its new (or perhaps disguised) form, this buddy relationship was beginning to move from children's programming into programmes that were predominantly targeted at youth.[20]

The puppet's interruptions, mugging to the camera, and apparently unscripted interventions all serve to enable the presenter to appear likeable, a good sport, and, perhaps, also more 'real' in contrast to his fluffy sidekick. In *MTV's Most Wanted*, the camera has taken the puppet's role, and appears to be friendly and deliberately self-reflexive, thus providing opportunities for jokes, and for an unrehearsed live feel that is not dissimilar to many actual puppets' roles.

The camera–presenter interaction within yoof programmes, therefore, did not instigate a new relationship between viewer and programme, but revamped, through parody, a familiar and pervasive aspect of television address. In this way the illusory aspects of the para-social relationship constructed within yoof television was made more, not less, visible. This visibility was further supported by the discourse of the presenters. In one episode of *Most Wanted*, Ray observed that his job as a VJ (video jockey) was both strange and banal. As he explained it, in the reality of the studio his job involves him talking into a camera through which he pretends to see out of, and into, the viewer's home (or viewing environment); this was, of course, actually an impossibility. At the same time—since *Most Wanted* was a Europe-wide request show—Ray was also simultaneously talking to people he could not see (many of who were not just in different cities but in different countries), on a telephone that he did not dial himself. In addition, the telephone itself was not visible on screen, and had no presence in the studio other than as an electronic link to Ray's hidden earpiece. Ray's relationship with viewers—individually on the phone or in his address to the viewing audience—was therefore entirely virtual, and it was a necessary act of faith for the audience, and for Ray, that he was talking to, and being seen by, them. Although Ray's self-reflexiveness is not unique to this genre of programming it certainly became one of the most distinguishing characteristics of the 'yoof TV' presenter's style. Antoine de Caunes, for example, the presenter of the music magazine show *Rapido*, as well as the smutty magazine show *Eurotrash*, is another exponent of this kind of archly self-reflexive pose. Similarly, presenters such as Dominik Diamond (*Gamesmaster*), Johnny Vaughan (*Moviewatch*,

---

20 I would argue that the success of 'Flat Eric', the yellow monkey-like puppet in the recent—1999—Levi's commercials, owes some of his success to many of the earlier fuzzy friends I mention here.

The Big Breakfast), and Chris Evans have all had instances where they direct the viewers' attention to how the programme is being made, and to the artificiality of their own position.

In *The Big Breakfast* the fluctuating presence/absence of the camera crew and support personnel, as well as the subversion of technology within the show also revealed the making of the programme to the viewers watching at home. Charlie Parsons, the original producer for the show, was explicit about the radical intention behind these and other aspects of the programme's deconstructive activity:

> This is going to sound like it should be in inverted commas, but *The Big Breakfast* was deliberately designed to deconstruct TV, in a way, it actually affects the way you see other TV programmes . . . When Chris Evans picks up a banana and talks into it rather than a telephone, it makes you look at *Going Live* in a different way, because they still pretend with the telephones.[21]

Parsons is not quite accurate about other TV programmes; in *Going Live*, while 'real' telephones were used for celebrity interviews, one of the presenters—Sarah Greene—often abandoned the real technology in favour of friendlier substitutes. During one of the interactive computer game items—which involved a simulated seabed and fish—Greene would use a seashell (as a substitute telephone) to talk to the young viewers phoning in to take part. It is true, however, that the deconstructive pose within the early days of *The Big Breakfast* was particularly pronounced, specifically because Chris Evans's presentation style was excessively self-reflexive. At numerous points in the programme he would point to the script, make comments about its quality, or snatch the hastily scribbled prompt boards from personnel crouching down under the camera he was addressing, thus disrupting the programme's apparent continuity, as well as his own role as narrator.[22]

The motivation behind this kind of style stems from a variety of reasons; one of the most pragmatic being that it allows for real as well as rehearsed mistakes. This is something that, with younger, less experienced presenters and production staff, must at some time have been a very real possibility. While many of the presenters I have named are clearly experienced professionals, *Network 7* itself was characterized by endless rehearsed and unrehearsed faults. This included loss of transmission from outside broadcasts, the trials of dealing with the unpredictability of invited guests, as well as the

---

21 Charlie Parsons, quoted in McLellan, 'Down the Tube', 49–53.

22 This is a style he has continued to pursue in other youth programmes he has presented, most notably in the teatime series *TFI Friday* and is something I will return to in greater detail in the penultimate chapter which relates specifically to television performance.

vagaries of telephone polls, all of which could be accompanied by more mundane running faults, such as inaccurate cueing between items. Presenters, in these circumstances, were struggling to control the programme, and would therefore be likely to seize on a mode of performance that would allow for mistakes as 'part of the fun'.

Yet in other programmes this amateur pose was clearly a deliberate performance style. In these situations, the appeal would be for the audience rather than the presenter. If, as a generation that had grown up with television, they felt, as Scott suggested, that they knew 'how TV was made', to pretend otherwise—for the presenter to simulate a real relationship—would, as he had indicated, be patronizing. In their knowing appreciation of this self-reflexive form of presentation, the young audience could thereby comfortably enjoy different yoof programmes, as they seemed to acknowledge that their audience was too sophisticated to be taken in. But this form of presentation actually provided another route into the programmes. By believing that they were on a more equal footing with the presenters, viewers would feel that they actually had a more direct connection to them.

In terms of the spatial aspects of the programme (both real and imagined) the viewer was also encouraged to fantasize about, and invest in, the programmes in a similarly ambivalent manner. In *MTV's Most Wanted*, Ray expanded and defined the place of the studio through a series of cued sound effects; a drum roll to mark a pun, cheering to mark a celebration, or even, on one occasion, a toilet flush to accompany the pulling down of a map. The use of such sound effects could, on one level, be said to make the place of the studio more real, by giving three dimensions to a two-dimensional image. By creating an imaginary sense of volume, the sound effects reinforced the apparent visual depth within, or behind, the television screen. While the use of sound effects in this way is not particularly novel, what made it peculiarly yoof was its execution; the clumsy timing, as well as the choice of sound effects themselves, continually reminded the viewer that the studio was an artificial environment. Ray often commented when the effects were mistimed or inappropriate; viewers could not fail to know that the sounds were fake, and they would thereby be reminded that both the recording situation and the programme were self-consciously make-believe, and not to be taken seriously. Similarly, at the end of each episode of *Rapido* the fixed mid-shot of Antoine de Caunes—which featured between each segment of the programme—was often pulled back to reveal a visual joke. At the end of one episode, for example, it was revealed that although Antoine's upper body was respectably suited, he had, beneath his jacket, also been wearing a ballet tutu. His apparent front to the television audience was therefore exposed as only 'half the picture', thus making it clear that to invest in his façade as a serious presenter would be ridiculous. Yet, despite these and other disruptive elements, many young people continued to phone in and send letters to all the shows I have mentioned as if they were in a position to construct a real relationship with Ray, Antoine, Chris, and their different crew members. Yet they were not being fooled; rather, they were playing or joining in a kind of double bluff. The self-reflexive pose of the presenters, as well as the stylish antics of the visual elements, encouraged the audience to collude in the practice of an illusory intimacy that they simultaneously understood as make-believe.

If *Network 7* is properly the originator of the aesthetic that was taken up and developed by many youth programmes in the transition from 'youth' to 'yoof', MTV's programming—as I have demonstrated —also reproduced many of the same stylistic looks and tricks. And whilst MTV's audiences were actually quite small during the late 1980s and early 1990s, MTV was important in Britain for its impact on terrestrial programme makers and in the way that the yoof aesthetic was developed and recognized. MTV's visual style and aesthetic pyrotechnics accrued a specific importance because they were felt by programme makers and critics to be the source of a new kind of television that seemed, like other youth-oriented entertainment, to be dense, chaotic, loud, flat, empty, and technologically self-conscious.

MTV's prominence was such that it often seemed to stand in for, or express, everything—good and bad—about youth television in general. The initial strangeness and apparently archetypal nature of MTV allowed critics to speculate, often leading to hasty assertions that youth television was paradigmatically post-modern, or, more contentiously still, that it was revealing about the inherently post-modern nature of the television medium itself. This connection was made, primarily, because the perceived superficiality in the content of the programmes aimed at a younger audience was unfavourably associated with the flashy surface and apparent emptiness of this new television visual style. E. Ann Kaplan, for example, argued that:

> The new post-modern universe, with its celebration of the look— its surfaces, textures, the self-as-commodity—threatens to reduce everything to the image/representation/simulacrum. Television, with its decentred address, its flattening out of things into a network or system, the parts of which all rely on each other, and which is endless, unbounded, unframed, seems to embody the new universe; and within television, MTV in particular manifests the phenomena outlined by Baudrillard.[23]

---

23 E. Ann Kaplan, *Rocking Around the Clock: Music Television, Postmodernism and Consumer Culture* (London: Methuen, 1987), 44.

I would argue that the situation was actually more complicated. As a different way into the aesthetics and development of this new television genre or form, I have avoided the temptation of seeing the television screen as a mirror, or as all surface. Instead, by thinking about the places in which young people live, and the kinds of visual and verbal material they are familiar with, yoof programmes and MTV can be seen as meaningful and to be appropriate to the particular needs of their audience. In fact, it is clear that young viewers were encouraged, and did invest emotionally in particular programmes as if they were *places*—the networks of social relationships and understandings—that Massey describes. What is interesting is that they continued to do this, despite the fact that they clearly knew about the superficiality of television's address and the 'fake-ness' of the different places it constructs. It is therefore necessary to disentangle the post-modern aesthetic of some of the programmes from assuming that this must also imply a post-modern (in)sensibility on the part of the viewer.

In this, I am following the kind of analytic approach suggested by Margaret Morse's observations in her article 'An Ontology of Everyday Distraction', where, she suggests:

> The phantasmagoria of television and its analogs is thus to be imagined less as an escape to flickering shadows in the cave than as a productive force which shapes spatio-temporal and psychic relations to the realities it constitutes. [24]

What Morse suggests is that the flickering shadows produced by the television image are not simply entrancing, but act as a force which directs and shapes the temporal and psychic reality of viewers. From this perspective, youth-oriented programmes are not just an endless stream of glowing, transient images and sounds, but rather offer opportunities for the construction of fantasy and identity for the young viewer. This kind of activity has perhaps been part of what it is to watch television since the very beginning of television viewing; but for Generation X this relationship was both particularly intense and problematic. Specifically, the way that media images and sounds were used by these young people was not as a substitute for their real surroundings but as a *part* of their actual surroundings. In other words, the relationship between mediated worlds and the self was no longer about an escape from the real world, but an integral part of how the world is made sense of, and how it was consumed.

---

24 Margaret Morse, 'An Ontology of Everyday Distraction: The Freeway, the Mall, and Television', in Patricia Mellencamp (ed.), *Logics of Television: Essays in Cultural Criticism* (London: British Film Institute, 1990), 202.

> Older concepts of liberation in everyday life based on 'escape
> attempts' and figurative practices are no longer viable in a built
> environment that is already evidence of dream-work in the
> service of particular kinds of commerce, communication and
> exchange. [25]

If individuals could no longer experience the 'pre-televisual world
of politics, the street, or the market-place' then it is important to
re-evaluate the way in which television functioned for Generation X
as an essential, rather than illusory part of the construction of social
life. The relationship between media technologies and the young
viewer, listener, or player's sense of place, self, and community, is—of
course—still illusory in some aspects, but it is also a real one, in the
sense that it forms a crucial part of society's built and lived environment. In addition, this relationship facilitates and inspires the pos-
sibilities and limits that are encountered in the space of sociability,
fantasy, and imagination that are integral to a sense of identity.

This has always been true of media technologies to a certain extent,
but the pervasiveness and intimacy of these media became particularly pronounced during the late 1980s, both in terms of their actual
presence, as well as in an increasing self-consciousness about their
use and place in daily life. This change was frequently conceptualized
through the way in which technology was seen to have developed
in the last twenty years or so. The following comment from Bruce
Sterling, in his much quoted preface to *Mirrorshades: The Cyberpunk
Anthology* is an early indicator of how the technology, and our new
relationship to it, blurred boundaries, not simply between illusory
and real relationships, but between the body and technology:

> Technology itself has changed. Not for us the giant steam snorting
> wonders of the past: the Hoover Dam, the Empire State Building,
> the nuclear power plant. Eighties tech sticks to the skin, responds
> to the touch; the personal computer, the Sony Walkman, the
> portable telephone, the soft contact lens. [26]

Technology, and I would add specifically television, is now no longer
about 'seeing at a distance' or a wonder of any kind. By the late 1980s
and early 1990s, television no longer acted primarily as a representative or a reflection of a world that was happening somewhere else.
Instead it became 'sticky', making connections to every part of the
young person's world—at home, at school, and at play. Television—
for this generation—was part of their very earliest memories, part of
their present and future, and very few had ever lived without it.

---

25 Ibid., 213.

26 Bruce Sterling, *Mirrorshades: The Cyberpunk Anthology* (London: Paladin, 1986), p. xi.

Television's increasing appearance in different places—bedrooms, kitchens, airports, clubs, and pubs—spread the potential for its invasion into every aspect of young people's lives. As I have demonstrated, yoof programmes developed particular strategies to counter the way in which television had become banal and less than magical. Thus, whilst appearing to be more in control, young people were still being seduced by the places that television conjured up. In a similar vein, William Gibson, the originator of the term 'cyberspace' explains how he was inspired to envisage the 'cyberpunk':

> Video games weren't something I'd done much, and I'd have been embarrassed to actually go into these arcades because everyone was so much younger than I was, but when I looked into one, I could see in the physical intensity of their postures how *rapt* these kids were. It was like one of those closed systems out of a Pynchon novel: you had this feedback loop, with photons coming off the screen into the kids eyes, the neurons moving through their bodies, electrons moving through the computer and these kids clearly *believed* in the space these games projected. Everyone who works with computers seems to develop an intuitive faith that there's some kind of *actual* space behind the screen.[27]

The cyberpunk's intimacy with technology can be seen as an extreme version of this emerging relationship between humans and technology—or between identities and simulations. Yet I can not accept the implications of Gibson's observations without some reservations, or at least not as they might relate to television; while part of my argument suggests that there are times when viewers believe in the 'space behind the screen' there are also times when they do not. In fact it is exactly a mixture of belief and disbelief that characterizes the yoof TV aesthetic. It is an uneasy *play* between investment and alienation, between an outsider's distaste and detachment and the insider's investment and knowledge.

The childish investment in the fantasy world created by television —in its stars, presenters, and puppets, and the false intimacy produced by direct address—is open to parody in a variety of contexts; but, within yoof programmes, the play with the intimate places of television and the exposure of technology at work was particularly prevalent. Yet, as I have observed, this deconstruction of television by the programmes did not truly remove the potential for emotional investment in the programmes, stars, or fake places. Quite intense emotional excitement is generated in even the most self-conscious of audiences, just as there are probably a large number of children who

---

27 William Gibson, quoted in Sherry Turkle, *Life on the Screen: Identity in the Age of the Internet* (London: Weidenfeld & Nicolson, 1996), 265.

are perfectly aware of the manufactured illusion of television, but who are nevertheless prepared to enjoy the pretence without necessarily questioning it. As individuals enter adolescence, however, and become more directly responsible for the construction of a feasible and knowing identity—or for an acceptable presentation of self—they are increasingly obliged to negotiate specific social constraints that privilege certain tastes, attitudes, and ways of self-expression. In a society filled with the real, fake, mundane, and the almost magical, yoof television offered places from which Generation X could work, and play, at the social and cultural transition from child to adult.

3
Youth and Music on Television

POPULAR music on television in Britain has long been associated
with youth: the *Six-Five Special*, although not the first British
programme to feature popular music, was the first programme
designed to attract a youth audience. Its format, a magazine show
featuring interviews, filmed reports, and music, has remained basic-
ally the same to this day, with shows like *The Word* and *TFI Friday*
presenting a similarly rehearsed 'un-rehearsed' mixture of bands,
presenters, and youthful crowd who dance, heckle, and mingle on
screen. What I want to examine in this chapter is *why* popular music
is so important for the youth audience, and then relate this to the
difficulties and successes that television has had in representing and
sometimes apparently debasing this significant investment.

Popular music on television is known to encourage particular
kinds of 'identity-making', and the different image-music sequences
it produces create spatial and sensual narratives which colonize young
viewers' imaginations along with their living rooms and bedrooms.
However, I will also describe how the combination of television and
popular music produces surprisingly unwieldy images and awkward
sequences of music/image/performance. Such sequences may have
begun with Elvis, in a tuxedo, serenading a Basset hound (on *The
Steve Allen Show*), but they are equally evident in the early difficulties
produced by the 'live' appearance of a rave act on *Top of the Pops*.
These problems lead me to a series of related questions: Why is the 'fit'
between music and image often so uncomfortable in these and other
instances? How, or why, do bands and/or individual artists appear
to 'sell out' when they appear on television, if being in a band, or
producing music, often presupposes some kind of an audience, and is
always already a commercial decision? And why do arguments continue to rage about authenticity whether the conversation concerns
groups as diversely authentic as Take That and/or Nirvana? And
what does 'authentic' mean for different audiences and at different
times? Another equally interesting question might be why a live vocal
performance on *Top of the Pops* is so important when the audience,
presumably, is being encouraged to buy the record. Presumably, the

audience generally understands that it is a 'live' performance precisely because it has some perceptible *differences* from the record or the CD or the cassette?[1]

To unpack these questions I will investigate notions of identity, aesthetics, and performance, and look at those image-music sequences that seem to fit the music, as well as those that do not. What I wish to address, in particular, is how the music is exposed and composed by the television image. Furthermore, I argue that it is now possible to discern how the history, as well as the conscious and unconscious memory of individual viewers—who are television viewers often before they are music listeners—informs the construction and reception of each new image-music event.

I will begin from two places, or two image-sequences, that fit the music, or more accurately, *seem* to fit with the 'affective space' of the music they accompany. This concept of an affective space, created or sustained by the music is important because it encapsulates more than simply the sound of the music, or the physical performance of the musicians. It also includes the individual's experience—his or her participation in the music making process—and suggests that the experience of music can be understood to be the space, imagined and physical, that music occupies, or 'fills up' with emotion, feeling, and sense. In this situation, sense should be understood as a sensibility that is both tactile and cognitive. The image-music sequences I will describe orchestrate or flatten this affective space in ways that are concretely related to the fact that they are experienced through, and produced on, the medium of television.

The first of these sequences is a memory of mine that crystallizes for me some of the pleasures that are generated when watching and listening to music on television. The second sequence is a short clip from a heavy-rock music video that haunts a senior rock critic concerned about the 'death of rock'. My memory is this: some time in the middle of 1983, Tracey Ullman, the British comedienne, was having some success as part of a BBC show called *Three of a Kind*. During this period she released a song called 'Breakaway' which was a top ten hit. Ullman and two backing singers appeared on *Top of the Pops*, the BBC's long running music show, to perform the song. Ullman was dressed in a parody of a 1960s girl group style (like The Ronnettes, perhaps, or The Supremes). Her hair was backcombed into a kind of punky beehive, which also emulated and parodied the dress of a contemporary version of the girl group—the British group Bananarama. During her performance, I noticed something that at the time I thought was amazing; Ullman was singing into a hairbrush. My

---

1 This is surely exacerbated by the fact that since many singles now increasingly feature several different versions, the concept of the 'original' version is increasingly difficult to sustain.

surprise was not that she was miming and therefore not singing live, for at that time nobody sang live on *Top of the Pops*, and everybody knew this, but that she was using a hairbrush. This was, for me, more shocking than if she had used nothing, or had mimed badly—for what it revealed was that other people *did it* too—they sang along or mimed to their favourite records with hairbrushes. Perhaps like me, they did this in front of a mirror, and imagined themselves on *Top of the Pops*. What Ullman did was to take the domestic props of fantasy —the hairbrush, and the approximate, and poorly realized, style of amateur 'dressing up'—and use them literally to act out her pop star persona. Ullman was both pretending and being—she was dressed up to be a pop star performing on *Top of the Pops*, but she also *was* a pop star (albeit a short-lived one) who *was* appearing on *Top of the Pops*. It was a parody, but an embracing one, amplified by the nostalgia, or the 'nearly remembered' sound of the music, and by the institutionalized place of fantasy represented by the *Top of the Pops*' studio. While other viewers might have seen Ullman's act as disruptive, or conversely, just plain silly, for me it seemed a strangely authentic moment as well as an entirely appropriate one; for me, it both embodied and celebrated the myth that is *Top of the Pops*.

My second image-music sequence similarly condenses a wealth of 'symbolic currency'. It also attempts to emulate and draw upon various myths and performance rituals that have been tied into the visualization of popular music. In this instance, however, Greil Marcus (writing in 1992), describes an accumulating symbolic overload that leads, for him, to a waning of affect—to, in fact, the 'death of rock'. This is his description of a short sequence which features in the music video for 'Every Rose Has Its Thorn' by the Los Angeles heavy rock group Poison:

> Backstage, adoring fans looking at once giddy and scared,
> are huddled against the wall, as if pressed back by vibrations
> emanating from Michaels' [the lead singer's] forehead. He's
> flanked by two bodyguards—mountains of flesh with heads so
> blocklike they barely seem human, no expressions on their faces,
> just a readiness to smash apparent in the way that they move. It's
> slow motion. Though nothing is really happening, tension builds.
> The disdain on Michaels face, in his walk, is precise and studied,
> a parody of every rock-star swagger from Elvis to Jagger. No one
> is laughing, Michaels least of all . . . This tableau of worship and
> hauteur is staged, an advertisement carefully constructed out of
> clichés that have been pretested and presold. They need only to
> be rearranged to produce the proper response: Bret Michaels,
> in his role, could be Sebastian Bach of Skid Row or Axl Rose of
> Guns'n'Roses as easily as he is himself. The demonstration is

riveting nonetheless. It is a pornography of money, fame, and domination, all for no reason outside itself, and all based on the magic of music.[2]

The image-music event Marcus describes here, like the sequence I remembered above, involves both parody and performance, and it is also about the power of images and music together. While the former is embraced—with a little embarrassment—the latter is viewed with distaste as Marcus sees it as seductive and abhorrent—as pornographic. In the Poison video the fit between the song and the video image is seen as being too slick, too demonstrable, and for Marcus the music (the magic) is debased by the images. But both image-music sequences reveal different tensions at work in the representation of popular music on television, and at work within popular music itself. These are the connections between, and the contradictions within, performance and authenticity. Both image-music sequences also reveal that even the most seemingly straightforward television images in these sequences are 'saturated' with a flow of conscious and unconscious meanings. This saturation is related, in part, to the presence and affect of the music itself—a factor that I will go on to discuss in more detail—but it also results from the activity of the viewer who understands and experiences each sequence through his or her own visual and autobiographical memories. I understood Tracey Ullman's performance because I related to the myth of *Top of the Pops* in a particular way—partly because I am British, a woman, and had watched *Top of the Pops* for many years. Despite himself, Marcus was fascinated by the Poison video because he is imbued with the myth of the 'macho rocker'—possibly because he is an American, male, and a professional music critic.

This saturation of the television image by the sound and performance of popular music has been usefully determined by Jody Berland. She describes the process like this; over a period of time, throughout rock history, images, performances, events, gestures, and poses are:

used and re-used, and reimbued with meaning, until a single image flickering before us resonates with a whole cookbook of crystallized uses.[3]

This leads to a situation where this real and mythological history of uses produces a specific kind of viewing situation, or viewing experience.

---

2 Greil Marcus, 'Notes on the Life & Death and Incandescent Banality of Rock'n'Roll' (1992), reprinted in Hanif Kureshi and Jon Savage (eds.), *The Faber Book of Pop* (London: Faber and Faber, 1995), 740.

3 Jody Berland, 'Sound, Image and Social Space: Music Video and Media Reconstruction', in Simon Frith *et al.* (eds.), *Sound & Vision: The Music Video Reader* (London: Routledge, 1993), 32.

It all begins to come together before us. The nuances of the face, the texture of the rhythm, the elliptical narrative, the fast-moving polyphony of style, the self-reflective humour, the montage of hospitable quotation and re-enactment, the familiarity of references to something still generic, still somebody's, the generosity with which its images join us to our collective history, our collective paranoia, favourite symbols, cynicism, hope.[4]

How does this happen? While acknowledging the power of personal memories and fantasies, in order to disentangle these loaded images we need to understand how they are made up, how, in Berland's words, they 'come together before us'. Evidently, part of these images' symbolic currency must have something to do with the affective power of the music. If this is the case, then we must look at how music makes meaning as *music*, and pay attention to the unique sensual qualities of music as a form and as an activity.

One traditional (and largely sociological) argument suggests that popular music is important, or is affective because it reflects or articulates particular ways of being in the world. After all, popular songs are dominated by a concern with strong emotions or with a specific state of mind—with love, hate, despair, joy, and angst—from being in 'love' to being someone in particular. Thus popular music can be characterized as embodying a whole range of sentiments and politics from 'Love Me Do' (The Beatles) to 'My Generation' (The Who) in the 1960s, to 'Everything I do (I do it for You)' (Bryan Adams) to 'Cop Killer' (Ice-T) in the 1990s. Yet listing the titles of songs, or pointing to the subcultural groups associated with the various musical genres (whether they are teenage girls, mods, 30-somethings, or ghetto youths) does not seem to take the argument much further. It does not actually explain why music creates affect, it just demonstrates that it must do. This perspective actually does not say very much about the music at all; it does not, for example, point to what is specific about musical experience in itself—that is, what makes music different from novels, paintings, comics, and films, from eating, or from dressing in a particular way. Simon Frith has commented upon this particular critical impasse and tries to pursue a way forward from this kind of analysis. What he proposes is that instead of describing the way in which music apparently reflects certain groups, it would be more useful to attempt to demonstrate how the music

produces them, how it creates and constructs an experience—a musical experience, an aesthetic experience—that we can only make sense of by *taking on* both a subjective and collective identity.[5]

4 Ibid., 32.

5 Simon Frith, 'Music and Identity', in Stuart Hall and Paul du Gay (eds.), *Questions of Cultural Identity* (London: Sage, 1996), 109.

From this perspective, he suggests:

> The aesthetic, to put this another way, describes the quality of an experience (not the quality of an object); it means experiencing *ourselves* (not just the world) in a different way. My argument here, in short, rests on two premises: first, that identity is *mobile*, a process not a thing, a becoming not a being; second, that our experience of music—of music making and music listening—is best understood as an experience of this *self-in-process*. Music, like identity, is both performance and story, describes the social in the individual and the individual in the social, the mind in the body and the body in the mind; identity, like music, is a matter of both ethics and aesthetics.[6]

From this perspective, music is no longer an object 'out there' which is somehow mapped back on to various groups and individuals, but is a practice, or an emotive force that is both within and without the individual subject. Music, then, is not simply reflective (either of its 'author' or its audience) but productive. This means that the acts of listening, playing, and dancing to music are creative acts in themselves. They are part of the way in which individuals engage in the process of identity-making. Music therefore creates affect for the individual because it offers a way of expressing, or, more precisely, because it offers a way of performing identity—of 'being oneself'. Of course, music is not a totalizing force in this process. For example, you might not necessarily expect music to create affect in this way during your supermarket shopping trips. Interestingly, however, it might, if inadvertently you find yourself listening to muzak as you peruse the aisles, or if you are wearing a Walkman and have thereby chosen your own particular landscape of sound.

In relation to a youth audience, however, Frith's arguments become particularly significant. In the context of my discussion concerning youth and identity, popular music's important position in young people's lives will be linked to the fact that it offers a powerful way of producing identity. Furthermore, popular music negotiates a relationship between the collective—the social, the public—and the individual—the personal and the private.

The co-option of music by television is therefore of consequence for youth in general. However, the way in which popular music was carried, or promoted, by the television image is distinctive in relation to the specific viewing context of Generation X. Since their negotiation of a public self/private self dichotomy has already been understood to have been overdetermined and, at times, overwhelmed by media, the (ab)use of music by a medium such as television was

6 Ibid., 109.

something to which Generation X were likely to be particularly sensitive. Programmes such as *The Word* and *Snub* were designed and positioned in a very deliberate way so as to counter this overdetermination. The fact that the two programmes use distinctly different visual and aural tactics to do so is explored in detail later on in this chapter.

At this point, however, I am still failing to *listen* to the music. For any music fan there is also a 'something else' or something 'more' that needs to be said, or understood about the experience of popular music. In relation to television, for example, it is clear that music does not offer the same *kind* of aesthetic experience as television. Otherwise, music and television would always fit together, and this, evidently, is not always the case. Instead, it is obvious that music and image *do* something to one another. Together they create a sensual narrative that is either more or less than the experience of music in a different context, whether this is at a live concert, on a record, or inside your head. Whilst Greil Marcus's comments indicate that television debases the music, Jody Berland's comments and my own experience suggest that music, in turn, also does something— saturates—the television image. To quote Frith again:

> There was always an excess in musical experience, something unreasonable, something that *got away.*[7]

However tempting it may be to conclude that the creation of musical affect is simply something unreasonable (and therefore unknowable) it is not only the something extra within musical experience that makes it different. Music is materially different from other kinds of aesthetic experience; it has a unique impact on the individual's corporeal, temporal, and spatial understanding and on their sense of self. This makes it very different from television. Below, Jody Berland describes how the television viewer and the music listener are situated differently. How, in fact, their respective experiences of space and time, and thereby their sense of place, are made distinctive by the way in which each form asks the individual to pay attention in a different way:

> While music fills a space and surrounds you in it, functioning as an extension of your body into the social, and vice versa, television attempts to surround itself with you, to draw your eyes into a single spot and to fix the rest of you before it. In the sense that its images transport you (via your eyes) out of the space that you are actually in, it does extend your reach in space, as McLuhan claims all electronic media do.[8]

---

7 Ibid., 116.

8 Berland, 'Sound, Image and Social Space', 36.

Television and music produce different kinds of spatial relationships. Music, literally or materially, becomes part of the space it occupies, and words that describe our experience of music make this clear—music reverberates, it is resonant, it vibrates, it can boom—it 'fills the space'. Like Frith, Berland also notes how this space is not simply the space around the individual—that is what appears to be out there or outside the body—but is, instead, both inside and without, as music articulates the 'body into the social, and vice versa'. Familiar words describe how music infiltrates our sensual self and our bodies. Music can be piercing (our eardrums), it can thud (making the body vibrate), it can be, asks to be, absorbed—whether this means sitting still with eyes closed, or expansively as the body pulses with a musical beat, as we tap our feet, or sway and dance. Sara Cohen describes this process in relation to 'Jack', an elderly man who forms part of her study of the musical activity (listening/producing/playing) undertaken by the Jewish community in Liverpool:

> Furthermore, although movement has been discussed in relation to music, movement is intrinsic to music. As non-verbal sound, music contains its own time and space, and it is experienced physically within the body, defining an inner, as opposed to an outer, space—although any natural relationship that might exist between music and body is of course culturally and historically conditioned. Many writers have suggested ways in which music communicates emotional states and processes upon which the imagination can act. This quality of music enables Jack to locate himself imaginatively within, or in relation to, different times or worlds, places and spaces, whether they be private or public; familiar or strange; feminine or masculine; sacred or profane.[9]

What Cohen is suggesting is that it is important to remember that music makes sense to us not simply because it articulates the social or the emotional but also because it is physical. Music can be seen and is felt to have a tangible effect that is more than, or different from, television. Attentive or absorbed music makers who perform, listen, or dance to the sound have a very different understanding of where they are, or where they imagine themselves to be, from the television viewer. From this perspective, it is not surprising that the potential experience offered by each form often makes them incompatible—music can touch its listeners in a way that television generally cannot.

While this interpretation has some merit, I feel that Berland's conclusion relies upon a too limited conception of the television viewer

---

9 Sara Cohen, 'Localizing Sound', in Will Straw *et al.* (eds.), *Popular Music—Style and Identity* (Montreal: Centre for Research on Canadian Cultural Industries and Institutions for IASPM, 1995), 65–6.

and underestimates the significance of the varied ways in which each individual can oscillate between different levels of attention. As I have suggested in previous chapters, it is clear that the television audience *can* shift physically and emotionally in relation to the television image. If the function of the television screen is no longer discrete, viewers will not always be cornered or transfixed by the television image—although of course, they may continue to be at certain moments. What I want to stress is that the distinction between the different spaces generated by music and television is not inevitable. The meaning of any televised music-image event cannot be dictated by surmising the essential (spatial) characteristics of each medium, just as meanings can never be completely determined by the conscious or unconscious intent that lie behind the production of different music-image sequences. Rather, it is because the experience of music and television is also dependent upon a certain temporal contingency—that is, what is experienced by the viewer/listener depends upon the particular time of viewing—that some music-image sequences can work for one viewer and not for another. It is also why some sequences feel 'right' for the same viewer at certain moments and then 'wrong' at others. If I were to see Tracey Ullman performing 'Breakaway' on *Top of the Pops* now, I would feel and make sense of the sequence very differently. Obviously, while it meant something to me then, it is not necessarily going to mean the same thing now—the fact that I associate the memory of the sequence with a series of self-conscious connotations is likely to make any re-viewing peculiarly fraught with potentially very different meanings.

But Berland does not suggest that the spatial aspect is the sole distinction between music and television. To return to Cohen's argument, music is different from television because in a very real sense, music is tactile, corporeal, in its effect. Using this to re-examine Berland's arguments, what is distinctive about music—rather than television—is that it can touch, or make a literal impact on the body at the same moment that it is also 'locating you imaginatively' elsewhere. Once more, it becomes obvious why the two forms are incompatible with one another. The material impact of television, with its relatively small screen and its limited production of sound, implies that music as experienced on television must always be circumscribed by the absence, or reduction of music's tactile qualities. Undoubtedly, this continues to be the case for many viewers; however, this position, too, relies heavily on ignoring the way in which, for many viewers—and particularly Generation X—the experience of television is as a primary rather than secondary medium. As Simon Frith suggests, the music listener is now often, initially at least, a television viewer, and in fact could be said to have 'learned to respond' to music from television itself.

It could be argued, in fact, that live audiences long ago learned how to respond to music from television—American programmes like *American Bandstand* and *Soul Train* and British programmes like *Ready, Steady, Go* and *Top of the Pops* were as significant in showing audiences as musicians at work.[10]

For Generation X and other audiences, television has become the primary (or original) source in the process of knowing about, and in feeling, the affect of popular music. The habitual, embedded nature of television within the experience of everyday life has resulted in a physically responsive, if not necessarily truly tactile, relationship with the 'box in the corner'. Generation X have grown up slapping, licking, waving, ignoring, gawking, and dancing in front of the television screen. They have often responded physically and emotionally in a way that is an even more intimate incorporation than that manifested by their parents, who themselves may have learnt, as Frith suggests, how to respond as a 'live' audience from different television programmes.

Nevertheless, music also continues to be situated, produced, and provoke responses that are not dictated—or originated—by television. When heard, danced to, or played elsewhere, music's 'sense-making' makes sense in a variety of different ways. What television programmes reveal is that there is rarely, if ever, only one place, or one appropriate (mental and physical) response to music. In fact, music can conjure up, or make sense, in a plurality of diverse places which television all too obviously attempts either to compete with or (inadequately perhaps) reproduce. The evident desperation in the rhetoric of various programmes when they proclaim the exclusive nature of certain musical performances—whether this was the 'hot' video on *The Chart Show*, the first appearance of a band on *Top of the Pops*, or a 'live and exclusive' satellite link in the same programme—indicate how anxious television is in its attempt to establish itself as the original site for musical experience. The construction of these music-image sequences as special, unique events indicates the way in which many music programmes try to present themselves, somewhat perversely, as accessible *and* exclusive. In these instances, television wishes to establish itself as the place where music comes from. By demonstrating that it can reproduce, or even create the appropriate response from the audience, television is being validated by the music, just as the music itself is privileged by its inclusion in particular television programmes—by the fact that it is *on television*.

So how exactly, does music appear on television? What is so special about the music-image event? What the combination of music and image attempts to restore, and even compensate for, is the fact that

10 Frith, 'Music and Identity', 225 n., 331.

the technology of television (along with film and other recording media) engenders a radical break-up in the structure of the real or imagined image-music-performance event. This has certain consequences for the way that popular music is produced and understood on television, which Jody Berland has described like this:

> The rise of modern media technology has been founded upon the separation of sound (in recording) and image (in photograph) and in their subsequent reunification through electronic means. The past sixty to eighty years have been propelled by two changing but inseparable processes of technical production: one which increasingly fractures the practices of making/recording/hearing/watching/visualizing music, and a second which reconstructs their relationship by artificial means.[11]

The original music event—a singer singing to an audience that is present before her or him in the same space at the same time—is taken apart by the recording and photographic process. It is then restored (or re-stitched) through the unification of sound and image on film or video, and thus appears to come together again in a version of its original form. Of course, while this version may be a simulation of an original musical event, it may even *be* the original event. This process of mediated restoration allows for at least three different viewing/listening positions to be organized for the television audience for various musical events. All of these have a different real or perceived relationship to the presupposed event that is taking place, and thus to notions of authenticity and affect in relation to the musical experience. Steve Wurtzler provides a useful table of the four possible positions for the music listener—as opposed to the television viewer—which is worth replicating here as Table 3.1. Of these four positions television can only reproduce II and IV. Yet, for the individual who wishes to privilege his or her *musical* experience, it is generally understood that as positions I and II are closer to an actual or original music event they would be the most desirable. They provide the opportunity to witness at first hand the skill of the musician and have a spatial and/or temporal proximity to the music making process. These positions are also the most likely to engender a situation where the 'something unreasonable' that Frith identifies can be located. This unreasonable quality is the auratic potential of music. This is where the uniqueness of music as a 'one and only', 'for now' experience is grasped for—or glimpsed, or felt. This auratic potential stems from the fact that music is experienced acutely in these situations as being ephemeral. By this I mean that the individual is made conscious that in listening, or responding to, the music, that what they are

11 Berland, 'Sound, Image and Social Space', 36.

TABLE 3.1. *Relationship of spectator-auditor to the 'event' posited by representation*

	Spatial Co-Presence LIVE	Spatial Absence RECORDED
Temporal Simultaneity	(I)	(II)
Temporal Anteriority	(III)	(IV)

Some Associated Representational Technologies/Practices
Position I.   Public address, vaudeville, theatre, concert.
Position II. Telephone, 'live' radio, 'live' television
Position III. Lip syncing, diamondvision stadium replays
Position IV. Motion pictures, recorded radio, and television[12]

experiencing is actually receding in time—as the beat goes on, or as the beat has gone. This promotes a 'never to be repeated' status for the music itself. Even if the same riff, or beat, or melody is repeated it can never be exactly as it was the last time. The physical and/or temporal co-presence of the audience with the 'source' of the music will therefore emphasize this aspect of the musical experience. At some level, the audience believes that in these situations there is an element of the performance that is uncontrolled, so that 'anything may happen'— intentionally or unintentionally. In positions I and II, therefore, the music experience will be closest to becoming the 'unique phenomenon at a distance', which Walter Benjamin identifies as the source of the aura in art works.[13]

Live situations, with their putative relationship to the original event, are therefore the locations where we expect the greatest or most powerful musical affect to be created, because they are the situations where the auratic qualities of the music are at their most intense. Yet the influence of recording and other electronic technologies on the music making process has increasingly led to situations, as Wurtzler suggests, where the quality, or the character of the aura in relation to the experience of music has necessarily been altered.

As socially and historically produced, the categories of the live and the recorded are defined in a mutually exclusive relationship, in that a notion of the live is premised on the absence of recording and the defining fact of the recorded is the absence of the live. Rather than the 'death of the aura' at the hands of mechanical or

12 In Steve Wurtzler, 'She Sang Live, but the Microphone was Turned Off: The Live, the Recorded and the *Subject* of Representation', in Rick Altman (ed.), *Sound Theory, Sound Practice* (New York and London: Routledge, 1992), 89.

13 See Walter Benjamin, 'The Work of Art in the Age of its Mechanical Reproduction', in *Illuminations* (London: Fontana, 1975).

electronic reproducibility, the recorded reinstates the 'aura' in commodity form accessible only with those events socially constructed as fully live.[14]

Liveness—and thus the determination of aura—has come to stand in for a 'category of authenticity completely outside of representation'. This has emerged from a situation where 'liveness' is primarily secured as an effect of a musical performance by conventions that suggest that it is not recorded rather than by any essential sense in which the event can be understood as being from the real. What this suggests is that authenticity—closely associated with the aura—is no longer guaranteed by the musical event itself, but with those historical and social conventions that discursively maintain a difference between the 'live' and the 'recorded'. These differences are maintained in order to inscribe the aura of the supposed original event on to the commodity, whether or not that commodity is a unit—a CD or cassette—or, in this context, the televised musical event. As Steve Connor observes:

> The live should be seen as a strategic category of the semiotic, even though its function *within* semiotic systems is to suggest that which lies authentically behind the distorting and falsifying operations of signification. The live is always 'produced' as an artificial category of immediacy, and is therefore a quotation of itself; never the live, always the 'live'.[15]

Even though, as Connor explains, the live performance must now be understood to be artificially constructed to appear 'live', the discursive conventions Wurtzler refers to enable the live performance to retain its heritage and thereby sustain the auratic potential of the music in specific contexts. How it does so, and whether it does so successfully, of course, will depend upon the conventions of the particular genre of music that is being performed.

Following on from this, we could imagine that television must predominantly feature 'live' musical performances. In practice, a lot of music on television is not experienced or produced in this way, and in any case it would not always be feasible. More commonly then, television often situates musical performance in a curious hybrid of positions II, III, and IV. *Top of the Pops*, for example, currently asks its artists to sing live. In doing so, however, they sing to a recorded backing track, and the show itself, and thus their 'live' visual performance, is recorded on a Wednesday to be transmitted on a Friday evening. On one level, this practice is understandable; it is likely that with the problems in controlling sound levels, the wish to avoid technical

---

14 Steve Wurtzler, 'She Sang Live but the Microphone was Turned Off', 89.

15 Steve Connor quoted in Wurtzler, ibid., 89.

glitches, and the need to allow for the vagaries of performers, producers try to control as much of the different performances as possible. Thus it is simply too risky, too inconvenient, and too expensive for television to reproduce a more unambiguously 'live' musical experience. Yet this desire to recreate or inscribe 'liveness' on to the musical performance on television is actually a convention. In the early days of *Top of the Pops* (in the 1960s) the fact that the music was always recorded, and never live, gave it a particular status and validity; the record—the vinyl single—was the important aspect of the music making experience. DJ presenters, such as Jimmy Saville, would actually put the record on a turntable on camera, before the band or singer performed. This kind of activity would be unthinkable now, and records have only appeared on *Top of the Pops* as part of the furniture of hip-hop performances.

Whilst not as glaring as the early days of *Top of the Pops*, there are still plenty of situations in which there is little attempt to reproduce the 'live'. In fact, what often occurs is a confusion, or blurring of the various positions Wurtzler identifies. Thus, for the television viewer watching music on television, there will often be a perceptible sense of dislocation resulting from an uncertainty as to what is 'live' about the performance they are watching. Or, perhaps, how *close* they actually are, physically, or temporally, in relation to the music event that is actually taking place.

In Wurtzler's argument the incident he concentrates on is Whitney Houston's performance of 'The Star Spangled Banner' at the 1991 American Superbowl. Although her performance—her physical presence, her tears and gestures—*were* live, her vocals were taped. This meant that her performance—her evident emotion—was open to question. If Whitney could 'fake' emotion in her voice—since the vocals were not a response to the live event but had been recorded earlier in a different context—might not her tears also be false?

In this and other circumstances, television seems inadequate in relation to musical experience because what it presents, in contrast to the live performance, are events that all too easily mislead the viewer. Even if events attempt to reproduce the 'live' they may fail to create the desired effect, as technical difficulties inhibit the reproduction of the live concert sound and atmosphere. Even the most faithful reproductions of live concerts can fail through a loss of transmission or poor sound reproduction. In fact, the pre-recording of Houston's vocal was apparently designed to guard against just such an eventuality.

Yet, the concern about what 'liveness' means in relation to musical experience privileges one aspect of musical affect over and above the experience of music and television *together*. And it is this that is the real subject of my investigation. In addition, as Wurtzler argues, many televised musical events are not a less than faithful record or representation of an original event, they *are* the event. Because of the way they are constructed—a combination of recorded sound, live performance, or recorded sound and recorded images—they are better understood not as 'originals', but as instances where there is, as Wurtzler suggests, a

> dismantling of any sense of an original event and the creation instead of a copy for which no original exists.[16]

Instead of concluding that television is unable to produce or guarantee an authentic musical experience for its audience, I argue that what we need to understand is how music and image work together to produce an experience that is affective in a spatial, gestural sense. Rather than searching for one version of authenticity—generated by the conventions of the 'live' performance—I will examine how the passage, or the slippage between different 'spectator–auditor' positions allows young viewers in to different but equally authentic musical–televisual spaces.

While Elvis Presley's appearance on American television produced one of the first instances of a conceivable 'mis-fit' between the musical performer and the television medium, this was perhaps inevitable (and ironic) in relation to his earlier appearances on *The Ed Sullivan Show*. For it was these earlier appearances which had demonstrated just what image, music, and television could achieve together. Jack Kroll recalls:

> It's no use sentimentalising this story, but it's important to feel something for the man whose great contribution was feeling. An immortal moment in our cultural history materialized on TV screens before 54 million people when Ed Sullivan, puckered with befuddlement, introduced 21-year old Elvis. 'I don't know what he does,' confessed Sullivan, 'but it drives people crazy.' And then Elvis was there, a baby slyness on his face, feinting once, twice, with his hips and guitar as the offscreen audience screeched each time, thinking he was going to start singing. And then he swivelled again, a Promethean twitch that brought a raunchy fire into the global village as he started to sing, 'You ain't nothin' but a hound dog.'[17]

Maureen Orth also remembers this moment. Significantly, she concentrates on its impact on the young audience watching at home:

16 Ibid., 93.

17 Jack Kroll, 'The Heartbreak Kid' (1977), in Kevin Quain (ed.), *The Elvis Reader: Texts and Sources on the King of Rock'n'Roll* (New York: St Martin's Press, 1992), 68–9.

After his famous first appearance on *The Ed Sullivan Show* in 1956, my aunt told me how foolish I was to sit screaming with joy at the spectacle of that vulgar singer on TV. It was then that I knew that she and I lived in different worlds, and it was then that kid's bedroom doors slammed all over America . . . Our parents hated Elvis and that was all right with us. From Elvis on, rock was rebellious.[18]

What is interesting about these observations is not simply that they describe one of the first and most significant instances when popular music on television had a significant impact in the homes and bed-rooms of America's teenagers. It is more interesting, for my purposes that it is a *remembered* event—both authors are writing in 1977, in response to the news of Elvis's death. In reinscribing a transitory televisual moment these writers reveal how the television image is saturated. Elvis's live performance is (mis)remembered in incredible detail, and then overlaid with a heavy inscription of myth—one that is 'Promethean', and when 'bedroom doors slammed all over America'. Evidently, as Jody Berland notes:

> some images are particularly potent. The image of the young-male-musician-with-guitar can mean, in a single flash, everything: bobby sox, punching out the boss, hitting the road, opposing the war, an old Chevy, 1958 in Kansas, dancing till dawn, coming on—this condensation of symbols coding the performance of a performer which can speak any of these without speaking at all.[19]

Over the passage of time and (as above) in retrospect;

> the image shimmers at the border of leaving the music behind, while celebrating itself as musically inspired.[20]

In other words, the burden of myth, the televised image of the Musician—whose gestures, swivels, and glances can mean so much —squeezes his or her music 'out of the picture'. This is what Greil Marcus, in his description of the Poison video is implying; not only is the image, he suggests, pornographic, he later claims that it is necrophiliac as well. This he argues is due to the legacy of Elvis as television star, which haunts every version of the 'rebel rocker'. For Marcus:

> This is where talk of the death of rock starts: with pointlessness surrounded by repetition. As two Paris critics put it in 1955 while

18 Maureen Orth, 'All Shook Up' (1977), ibid., 64.

19 Berland, 'Sound, Image and Social Space', 37.

20 Ibid., 37.

writing about the art world, it starts with the feeling that you're trapped in 'a dismal yet profitable carnival, where each cliché has its disciples, each regression its admirers, every remake its fans.' It's as if the source of the depression is not that rock is dead but that it refuses to die. Far more than Elvis, really, a clone like Bret Michaels, so arrogant and proud, is of the walking dead. It's just that the money's too good to quit.[21]

Ironically, Marcus is making this argument because he is still swept up by the carnival and goes on to claim that such deadly lust is mitigated by the intervention of the rock group Nirvana. Nirvana, he suggests, are able to create a splutter of meaning by 'going through the motions for a crowd as sick of the ritual as they are'.[22]

In this context, what is important is not really the authenticity of the music, but the ability of the audience to understand the significance of the images. Jody Berland elaborates on this point;

> The American media, feeding with the teeth of its own vocabulary, gathers to its centres a selection of recurring images whose serialized passage from source to resource endears itself to its audience, simultaneously making welcome its own transnational semiotic centralization. It creates a form of semantic flattery. The reproduction of symbols = the reproduction of competence = dependent pleasure.[23]

How did television reproduce such images for Generation X? How did youth programmes take their part in this process? How did they produce image-music sequences for a generation that was, as Marcus claimed 'sick of the ritual' and who may have been, as Larry Grossberg suggested, kids who know 'too much'.[24]

In the late 1980s and early 1990s, there were two specific ways in which British youth television produced musical performances. Both were designed to deal with a situation where the live was understood to be a conventional construct—as 'live' rather than live. One form of programming used parody, a knowing stance, and excess—a kind of 'saturation' overload. This strategy was particularly evident in a show like *The Word*. Another strategy, in contrast, tried to play down the importance of the image in the programme, deliberately reducing the visual element of the spectacle in order—apparently—to diminish

21 Marcus, 'Notes on the Life & Death', 743.

22 Ibid., 745. Written before Kurt Cobain's suicide, Marcus cannot have foreseen what effect Nirvana's success would have, and the tragic consequences for Cobain, who it seems, really did become 'sick of the ritual'.

23 Berland, 'Sound, Image and Social Space', 36.

24 Larry Grossberg, *We Gotta Get Out of this Place: Popular Conservatism and Postmodern Culture* (London: Routledge, 1992), 185.

its power. In these programmes the television images appeared raw and amateur, so that the music became the focus of attention. This was the strategy of shows like *Snub TV* and *The White Room* as well as, surprisingly perhaps, *The Hitman and Her*.

On British television the conventions of the youth music show had not greatly changed from the very earliest days of youth television. Here, for example, John Hill describes the set up of the *Six-Five Special*:

> [The] desire to cater to both young and old was already implicit in the show's early billing as the 'bright "new look" programme' aimed not simply at young people but 'the young in spirit of all ages'. It was also evident in the show's format, which was much more of a mix than is commonly remembered. This took the form of a cross between a variety show and a magazine programme, in which musical acts, of various kinds, were interspersed with comic turns and special items.[25]

This mix was echoed in the format of many youth music programmes (among them *Ready, Steady, Go* in the 1960s and *The Tube* in the 1980s), but reached its parodic apotheosis in *The Word*, the music magazine show produced by Planet 24 for Channel 4. *The Word* featured music but it also involved chat show elements (usually a young film, television, or sports star and an older British variety celebrity), special film reports (on Hollywood films, or covering international light news topics such as America's 'girl gangs' or Australia's 'Iron men'), variety acts (which included an act involving a condom being pulled through someone's nose), and different comic turns. It is ironic that this kind of mix was, according to Hill, originally designed to

> not only broaden the show's appeal, but also to temper, in the appropriate Reithian manner, the programme's offerings of entertainment with small doses of information and education.[26]

This is clearly not the intended effect when reproduced by *The Word*:

> Mark Lamarr's in charge of the sofa, which means tonight's interviews (with Chris Eubank, all ponced up in riding breeches and boots and Rolf [Rolf Harris], there to plug his 'Stairway to Heaven' cover) are funny and to the point. In between we've seen a designer porn queen play with an erection sculpted out of ice, and watched Rage Against The Machine get swamped under a writhing ruck of fans.[27]

25 John Hill, 'Television and Pop: The Case of the 1950s', in John Corner (ed.), *Popular Television in Britain* (London: British Film Institute, 1991), 92.

26 Ibid., 92.

27 Jim McLellan, 'Down the Tube', *The Face*, 54 (Mar. 1993), 53.

Despite the radical shift in the way in which the shows were perceived, the formal similarities between the two programmes can also
be seen in the inclusion of a lively and youthful audience. As Hill
notes, the inclusion of ordinary but hip participants, who did little
more than dance to the music, or respond to events in the studio, was
an important part of the *Six-Five Special*. Dancing, in particular,
was to become an important part of the show's success. The innova-
tion was not unique to Britain, however, as at least two American
shows, *American Bandstand* and *The Buddy Deane Show*, had already
demonstrated how successful such participants could be. Yet, by the
time of *The Word*, as I will go on to demonstrate, this audience is very
different from previous on-screen crowds, primarily because it is
clearly out of control and actively disliked by the show's presenters
and producers.

Initially, however, the on-screen audience was (and, despite the
resentment, still remains) one of the most significant ways music was
actively promoted and regulated by television. The movement of the
dancers, and literally seeing people react on screen, demonstrates
and embodies the physicality of the music. In the early days, dance
crazes, either openly taught to viewers or performed by the crowd,
revealed the prescriptive nature of some aspects of youth culture at
that time. As the fashion for such dances declined, most programmes
established a freer form of dancing by the audience. Their presence
guaranteed at least two things; firstly, that the music was meant to
have and demonstrably did have a physical as well as an emotional
affect, and secondly, that it had this effect on people who were
'ordinary', just like the young viewer at home. This second guarantee,
however, was sometimes challenged by the introduction of individuals who were paid to act as 'supra-representatives'. Both *Top of
the Pops* and *The Word*, for example, invited and employed professional or semi-professional dancers to work in the crowd (or
on separate, elevated platforms) to keep energy levels high, and to
provide guaranteed points of focus for the studio director. Employing professional dancers could mean that the music became less important, or carried less affect, as viewers realized that such dancers
could, or would, 'dance to anything'. Yet this could be mitigated by the
possibility that their viewing pleasure was increased, as the professional dancers were likely to be better at dancing, and were likely to be
more attractive than ordinary people. This could be characterized
as the 'Pan's People effect'. Pan's People were a much loved but much
ridiculed dance group who once performed weekly on *Top of the
Pops*, producing notoriously literal interpretations of current chart
hits. While their presence encouraged a certain amount of voyeuristic
pleasure in the audience, they were also seen effectively to trivialize

the music they performed to, whether it was Gilbert O'Sullivan or The Clash.[28]

Whether or not they were professional dancers, the presence of youthful representatives on screen meant that another elusive element of an authentic musical experience that was displaced when music was produced on television could be simulated. A young crowd, dancing and talking amongst themselves, rubbing shoulders with presenters, performers, and cameras was clearly meant to reproduce the sociability and the collective experience of music. As a crucial part of the televised event, edits were carefully orchestrated to include the on-screen audience into the structure of the song and performance. Watching archive footage of shows like *Top of the Pops* and *Ready, Steady, Go* reveals that the audience's presence, their proximity and affective reaction was used to try to fill in the gap between the performer separated—in time and/or space—from the television viewer. Their presence is a way of creating an imaginary totality between the event and the viewer at home. This is clearly the case in the sequence featuring Rage Against The Machine in *The Word* cited above; here the proximity and interaction between the audience and the band are an essential part of the music's impact as televised spectacle. The importance of audience as context also explains why rave acts often looked awkward on *Top of the Pops*. While there was always an on-screen audience in the *Top of the Pops* studio, the atmosphere and environment of a rave—established by thousands of dancers and perhaps an outside location—could not possibly be reproduced by a few star-struck teenagers herded close to the stage.[29]

While the on-screen audience remained useful to many youth music programmes, in some shows the perception of their role underwent a radical development. By comparing three contrasting descriptions of this on-screen audience at different stages we can see an increasing separation between the young television audience and the audience on screen. Initially, in their most powerful incarnation, such audiences were not dissimilar from the young dancers John Waters alludes to when he describes the cultural impact of *The Buddy Deane Show* in the early 1960s:

> You learned how to be a teenager from the show. Every day after school kids would run home, tune in and dance with the bedpost or refrigerator door as they watched. If you couldn't do the Buddy

28 Not surprisingly, considering *Top of the Pop*'s increasing concern to establish its credentials as a 'live' show, Pan's People and the dance groups that followed were dropped from the show in the early 1980s.

29 As dance music has become an established part of the mainstream music scene most dance acts now actually appear on *Top of the Pops* with their own dancers— effectively providing their own marginally more credible version of Pan's People.

Deane Jitterbug (always identifiable by the girl's ever-so-subtle dip of her head each time she was twirled around), you were a social outcast.[30]

By the time of Sean Cubitt's mid-1980s description of the on-screen crowd in *Top of the Pops* the young people on screen are no longer simply role models or representatives. Instead, their presence and their orchestration into the place of the *Top of the Pops* studio, produce a process of exclusion and inclusion for the young viewing audience. This works by establishing the differences between different family members who may be watching together. Cubitt describes the on-screen audience as they are produced through what he calls a 'classic' *Top of the Pops* shot. In such a sequence, he argues, the viewer at home witnesses:

> the camera moving either in or out from close up, to bring us all into the midst of the dancers. This is a very curious movement. It opens up a conflict between the shot's 'cinematic' function, of drawing the viewer in to the 'filmic' space, and the strictures of the domestic viewing space—which militate against identification in any traditional sense. Its purpose is to draw us in to the magical community of *Top of the Pops*, into that wonderful world without parents. But if the camera draws us in, the family pulls us out.[31]

Here, and elsewhere in his argument, Cubitt suggests that the 'politics of the living room'—the domestic viewing context where parents and older siblings are also present, along with the directly addressed young viewer—threatens any easy process of identification. Through their comments, jokes, and sneers, grown ups pull the young viewer continually back into the domestic context away from the fantastic, magical community suggested by the space of the *Top of the Pops* studio. The fragile investment Cubitt describes here thus marks a definite change from the unabashed process of identification that Waters's Baltimore teenagers expressed. Nevertheless, it demonstrates how the on-screen crowd did more than decorate the studio. They are an important part in the inscription, or the 'making up' of the magical place of *Top of the Pops* as a broadcasting institution.

While there is still a residue of this effect even today—and not only in *Top of the Pops*—there has been another development. By the time of *The Word* in the 1990s the 'nicest kids' were superseded by the kind of young people described below by *The Word*'s producer, Paul Ross:

30   John Waters, 'The Nicest Kids in Town', reprinted in Kureshi and Savage (eds.), *The Faber Book of Pop*, 152.

31   Sean Cubitt, 'Top of the Pops: The Politics of the Living Room', in L. Masterman (ed.), *Television Mythologies: Stars, Shows and Signs* (London: Comedia/Routledge, 1984), 47–8.

I just don't like the cut of their jib. They turn up and drink our beer, they smell funny and look scruffy . . . If I could, I'd arm my floor manager with cattle prods to jib those cunts around. They're there as sheep and they should know it.[32]

While such invective has to be understood as a deliberate pose, it is clear that what Ross is doing is trying to establish a *difference* between the studio audience and the television audience. McLellan is careful to note, for example, that while Ross is happy to produce streams of 'soundbite venom' in relation to the on-screen audience—who in their general rowdiness are likely to have caused him some very real headaches—he tells us that Ross

does seem sincere when he says that really he has no idea who watches *The Word* (3.5 million people do), that he loves them for just tuning in.[33]

Pragmatically, of course, as a television producer, it is the television audience and not the studio yobs who keep Ross in work, and Ross is therefore not in the business of alienating his viewers—although he does intend to shock them. Yet, I suspect that Ross is also aware that this generation of young viewers perceive the on-screen audience rather differently from before. A familiarity with television, and with the ritual presentation of music on television, along with the prolif-eration of minor celebrity status conferred by the mass medium, led to a certain uneasy contempt on the part of Generation X for their on-screen counterparts. From their perspective it is all too likely that these ordinary kids are, in fact, not really ordinary, but wanna–bes who can and want to become incorporated into the inauthentic world of television. More worryingly, in the case of *Top of the Pops*, they may also be (or have been) your parents. This is something that the producer/writer Danny Baker demonstrated, when he presented an anniversary special on *Top of the Pops*. Baker took time out in the show to reminisce how he had once been part of the on-screen audi-ence for the programme. He even went as far as to find archive footage of the back of his own head. The heritage of some music programmes therefore creates a situation where the magical aspects of an illusory, glamorous community no longer seem fantastic, but are revealed as curiously empty, and rather easy ambitions. Where, to amend The Rezillos' song, 'Everybody's *been* on *Top of the Pops*'. This erasure of the necessary tension between inclusion/exclusion—so that parents, for example, may no longer sneer, but look for, or reinscribe them-selves into the studio audience—effectively dissolves the 'politics of

32 Quoted in McLellan, 'Down the Tube', 53.

33 Ibid., 53.

the living room'. Thus the exclusive territory and place of youth—in this case the *Top of the Pops* studio—has been given up.

This suspicion that everything—even being in the audience—has been done before is particularly acute for young viewers who were born after the supposedly most authentic or powerful generations of the youth-music-spectacle. Generation X were born too late, whether this was the moment when Elvis made rock rebellious in the 1950s, or the myth of the swinging and radical 1960s. The sense of missing out, and an encroaching resentment and cynicism about the exploitation of the mythology of youth culture, was particularly intense for Generation X. Growing up in the late 1980s, they were not only obliged to carry the weight of a nostalgia for the 1960s, but also grew up in the aftermath of the apocalyptic 'No Future' prophesied by Punk in the late 1970s. Punk had been defined—in part—by its attempt to establish itself as the last authentic youth-music rebellion, and it did so by suggesting that any remaining mythological connection between rock, rebellion, and youth had reached its nihilistic endpoint in the lucrative excesses of commercial exploitation. Malcolm Mclaren's title for the Sex Pistols film—*The Great Rock'n'Roll Swindle* (1980)—made this aspect clear in a suitably heavy-handed way.

Punk was, of course, not the end of the relationship between youth and popular music, and commercial concerns as well as the subcultural activities of young people recreated some myths out of necessity.[34] None the less, it was not an option for this specific generation to invest wholeheartedly in commercially mediated representations of youth and music. Any unguarded emotional investment could easily be exposed as being both naïve and unsophisticated.

Unsurprisingly, this resulted in a form of cynicism which, in the case of *The Word*, was directed towards the studio audience, as well as (in most cases) the presenters too. This was made clear in the press coverage of the original presenters, Terry Christian and Amanda de Cadenet. Here, Amanda, in an interview with both her and Terry for *Q* magazine, responds to a question about how much money she earns.

> *Fucking hell!* People slag us off *anyway.* If they knew how much we got paid, they'd just say, god, they get paid *that* much to be so *crap*?[35]

Increasingly, *The Word*'s studio audience was also demonized as talentless wanna-bes who 'didn't give a fuck'. Yet, like Amanda, they still sought and succeeded in achieving celebrity status. Thus the

---

34 The use of 'new' in subcultures formed in the early 1980s in Britain indicates a desire to break with the past—as in 'New Wave', 'New Pop', and 'New Romantics'—although in fact all of them relied heavily on previous fashions and musical styles.

35 Amanda de Cadenet, quoted in Tom Hibbert, 'What the Hell does *The Word* Think it is?', *Q* (Mar. 1992), 7.

on-screen audience—rather than becoming a focus for a form of fantastic investment by the television viewer—was reinvented as a 'false' representation of youth. As the series progressed, it became clear that they were figures whom the audience at home was encouraged to define themselves *against*. Ultimately, as a focus for this kind of derision they were encouraged to humiliate themselves by agreeing to eat slugs, or bathe in eels, or drink offal milkshake. This was in *The Word*'s most notorious item, 'The Hopefuls', where supposedly ordinary young people were unadvisedly grabbing a chance at fame by appearing on television in any guise whatsoever. This victimization of the studio audience could only be understood—or enjoyed —from the perspective of a jaded television viewer. For what the hopefuls were doing wrong was to invest openly and unwisely in the commercially polluted and largely debunked fantasy of fame and glamour putatively established and authorized by television.

The derisory behaviour of the studio audience was, however, largely detached from the way in which the musical performances were incorporated into the show's environment. Although the studio audience's reaction to the music was often excessive it is surprising that the relationship between the studio audience, the musical performers, and the music itself, remained largely unchanged since the practices of the earliest music magazine programmes. In *The Word*, just as in the *Six-Five Special*, as well as *Ready, Steady, Go*, bands and singers who appeared on the programme were placed in close proximity to the studio audience. In all three shows, in fact, there was a clear similarity in the way in which the place of the studio was orchestrated for musical events. Performers were either raised on platforms or on the studio floor. They were then surrounded by a gaggle of shifting audience members who fluctuated between pleasure in the performance, excitement at being on television, or cool disaffection. The two later shows also featured visible roving cameras that were forced to negotiate a path through, between, and, in *The Word*, over the top of, the crowd.

This intimacy between performers and audience often bolstered the musical performance. Conversely, it also served—excessively in *The Word*—to confuse the performers who would often find themselves juggling uncomfortably between looking and reacting to the studio audience, while simultaneously attempting imaginatively to look at, and perform for, the viewer at home. This was a particularly fraught process as the demands of camera, crowd, and even the emotional structure of the song were often in competition with one another, leading to a situation where the singers, in particular, literally might not know what to do with themselves.

In other shows such difficulties were more directly controlled. One way was simply to allow more time for a rehearsal; *Top of the Pops*, for example, had time by recording on a Wednesday and transmitting on the Friday, either to re-record, or to edit out, any glitches in a group's or singer's performance. In addition, in other shows the mode of address adopted by the musician and the behaviour of their audience were more carefully connected to the status of particular performers and with different types of song within specific genres.

Yet, despite *The Word*'s apparent chaos, there were some very familiar conventions at work. In particular it was in the visual effects employed to support the music that this could be seen. In *The Word* the visual geography of the studio was transformed in response to the music, although the actual space of the studio remained the same. As I have described, in the cramped, deliberately overcrowded studio, musicians were often obliged either to perform right next to mugging audience members, or in inappropriate pieces of set. In one programme, the soul singer Adeva was obliged to perform in the confines of a wrestling ring which had been set up for a comic item later in the show. Instead then, of a fixed, designated area, the space made for music in the show was, in almost all cases, virtual. As each band or singer performed on the programme the white background of the studio was covered—for television viewers—with a wash of acid-coloured light effects (through the technique of Colour Separation Overlay) which distorted or removed the dimensions of the studio. These non-representational bands, stripes, dots, circles, and blobs of colour moved and vibrated—not necessarily in time with the music—and effectively destabilized the dimensions of the studio by replacing the apparently fixed white background—the walls of the studio—with a virtual, depth-less scene. With a heaving crowd and with the cameras either submerged within the mêlée or swooping over the top of the participants, this musical, visual spectacle made the music special, while continuing to create a sense of dislocation and confusion. While the otherwise generally conventional framing of the band or artist might be seen as an attempt to ground the viewer, this was often lost due to the frenzied activity of the crowd and confusion inspired by the lighting effects. Ultimately, the result of the visual effect was to distort, or even destroy the previously established dimensions of the studio as a place. For the viewer at home, the explosion of colour, and a sense that the space of the studio had expanded (since the walls had disappeared), could also be associated with the affective and expansive nature of the music. It also echoed the colour and chaos of the contemporary club scene. While such effects also bore some resemblance to backdrops used predominantly by 1960s bands—who wanted to infer or reflect drug use[36]—the acid

36 I recall that a televised performance of the song 'White Rabbit' by Jefferson Starship employed a similar version of this backdrop.

wash employed by *The Word* worked primarily to establish the musical performances as distinct from the rest of the show. This visual over-compensation was designed to allow or alert viewers to invest in these moments in a less cynical way than they did to the rest of the show's contents. Mark Lamarr, who co-hosted the show for a couple of series, articulated this sensibility when he was quoted as saying that while he did not watch the rest of the programme, he did tape the show so that he could 'fast-forward to the bands'. This attitude, along with the later development of a condensed version of the programme—*The Word: Access All Areas*—which featured the music and additional backstage footage at the expense of some of the racier magazine items, confirms that despite its deliberately camp attitude, the programme used music as a focus for sincere investment by the young viewer.

Other programmes used different strategies so that Generation X could take music seriously yet remain detached from television itself. One of the most critically successful series bought by the BBC for the youth audience was the independently produced music show *Snub TV*. *Snub*'s format consisted of extremely low budget videos, filmed reports, and interviews segmented together in a short half-hour programme interspersed with the trademark *Snub TV* eye, blinking—or winking—slowly between each item. Clearly a human eye, the pupil was replaced with the *Snub TV* logo hovering over the iris.[37] Although the items within the programme were nominally held together by a female voice over, there were no presenters on screen to make a link between each segment. During interviews, questions were posed off camera by the 'editor/producer/interviewer' Brenda Kelly and/or her partner, Peter Fowler.

Reviewing the publicity and press coverage relating to the programmes demonstrates that *Snub*'s credibility was determined in part by two factors. Firstly, both Fowler and Kelly had originally worked in the 'independent' music sector rather than the television industry, implying that they were not only insiders in relation to the music business, but also more likely to take the music rather than the televised aspect of the show seriously. Secondly, the programme was cheap to produce—a fact consistently highlighted by practically all the press coverage for the programme. The low cost of the show aligned it with a particular version of authenticity and was identified in this way by several reviewers. Commenting on Janet Street-Porter's editorial decision to buy the show, Colin Shearman, writing in the *Guardian*, writes:

> Funnily enough though—and here Ms. Street-Porter's possible genius comes into play—this shoe string budget has forced them

---

37 This obviously has an echo of the *i-D* 'wink' I discussed in the last chapter.

[Kelly and Fowler] to evade many of the blunders that plague other music programmes. Interviewing guests themselves, for instance, not only saves money but also—since they ask their questions off camera—helps focus on the music rather than the ego of the presenter. 'And since we can't afford to invite groups into the studio, it's just a matter of "tell us where you'll be at 4 o'clock and we'll turn up and do the interview there"' adds Kelly. Seeing musicians on their homeground like this—backstage after a gig perhaps—produces a good atmosphere and makes it much easier to coax relaxed interviews out of people who've possibly never been on television before.[38]

Shearman makes several interesting associations here; firstly that the 'shoe string' budget, rather than being detrimental to the image, actually guarantees that the image is presented with a lack of pretension. Secondly, money constraints also mean that music makers are sought out in their appropriate environment—backstage at gigs—rather than being confined within the supposedly artificial environment of a television studio. Interestingly, these are factors that originate off screen and are then read on to the image itself. Shearman even indicates that this means that *Snub* regenerates what is often vaunted as the essential purpose of the television image—that it can transmit, unadorned, raw visual information. It is this sense of immediacy and revelation that Shearman romanticizes when he refers to 'people who've never been on television before'. All of this constructs the programme as having an authentic media naïveté and allows the interviewees and the programme the privileged position of somehow being outside of the contaminating 'media loop' described by Jody Berland.

The visual aspects within the programme evidently attempted to reflect these associations. One item from the 1990 series focuses on the group New Order; beginning with footage of the band members backstage, crammed into a dressing room, they are interviewed with the camera and the sound boom clearly visible in shot. In this instance the camera and boom are apparently inadvertently reflected in the dressing room mirror that is behind the band members. The interview is then inter-cut with 'live' concert footage of the band. The informality of the presentation and the sense of intimacy that all of this implies engenders a feeling that the band and their music are being seen in a way that is as raw and real as it is likely to get on television. Yet the show's rough and ready pose, and its cutting edge rhetoric actually depend a great deal on the suggestiveness and conventions of 'live' performance. Firstly, in terms of the representation of musical performances—which I will describe in more detail below

38 Colin Shearman, 'More Pop and Less Champagne', *Guardian*, 23 Mar. 1989, 28.

—and secondly, on the reproduction of a form of investigative television journalism. In this kind of television, technical flaws—such as the camera and boom being in shot—are actually inscribed into a visual ideology which interprets the camera's presence as a hallmark of *verité* or truthfulness. In other words, the visibility of the recording technology functions not as a production error, but as an indicator of the deliberately unstructured, and thereby undistorted status of the event being recorded.

Such unstructuredness should result in a diverse form of presentation. Yet examining *Snub*'s coverage of three different bands' musical performance reveals that the footage of the Jesus and Mary Chain, The Stone Roses, and The Happy Mondays actually demonstrates a fair amount of uniformity in the way they are presented. Even given the fact that all three bands fall loosely into the 'indie' genre, they are constructed by the programme through very similar and very conventional ways of coding authenticity and liveness. Indeed, they provide clear instances of how Wurtzler's notion of the 'live' and its associated appeal to authenticity is being reproduced by television. All three items on the bands feature some concert footage which, as the voice over constantly reminds the viewer, has been recorded 'live'. This is despite the fact that each sequence clearly demonstrates the results of an extensive post-production process. In addition, in all the sequences, the lighting of the television image is primarily dictated by the stage-lighting of the live show. This produces contrasting and sometimes blinding switches between light and shadow, with the singer and musicians alternatively silhouetted, obscured, and/or bathed in strong coloured lights that are predominantly white, red, or purple. At certain points in each song, often during the instrumental sequence, the lighting flashes rhythmically; an effect sometimes clearly generated by strobe lighting. This produces a visual rhythm that at different moments appears to coincide and sometimes work in counterpoint with the rhythm of the music. In each of the three sequences the lighting is used illustratively, in close relation to the rhythm of the music. This serves to sanctify or dramatize the main participants on stage; at other times it attempts to swamp and include the on-screen audience by flashing over them, or draw them in at specific moments of climax. For the viewer at home, this process is also encouraged by the use of basic video effects, such as the slowing down or repeating of the image, a degrading or 'pixelating' of the focus, and a bleaching or saturation of certain colour ratios. This latter technique is particularly evident in the item featuring The Happy Mondays.

The basic mechanics, or shot by shot structure of each 'live' sequence is also very similar in all three items on the different bands. In all three of the performances, a crucial element is the inclusion of a heaving and predominantly male audience who either mug to the camera or move their heads and arms in time to the music. These sequences are then intercut with shots of the band on stage, with a majority of the images concentrating on the lead singer. Although there are close-up shots of the drummer and the lead guitarist, they are always employed at moments where, musically, their contribution is most apparent: during a guitar break, or where the rhythm of the song is particularly emphasized. This, in turn, means that less self-evidently participant band members—such as the bass guitarist for example—generally receive much less attention. Bez, the on-stage dancer of The Happy Mondays, is the exception to this rule; but this is surely because he effectively embodies the physicality of the music and is substituted, at key moments, for the on-screen audience, as he dances away in his characteristically 'drugged up' fashion. In contrast to Bez's 'full on' exposure, in all three items shots which feature the lead singer *singing* usually focus exclusively on his upper body and use extreme close-ups of his mouth pressed close to the microphone. Such shots effectively pull the viewer in, close to the vocal, just as the song's structure also emphasizes this aspect of the singer's performance. When a slight deviation from this occurs in the item on The Stone Roses—where the lead singer is framed so that his whole body is on display—this is, I suspect, because Ian Brown (the lead singer) has a curious rocking dance. By swaying and contorting himself to the music, he effectively almost cradles the microphone. This distinctive pose, apart from representing the singer's own apparent intensity, is also suggestive of a physical response that visualizes the unique emotional and physical power of the music.

While in all three items many of the crowd shots were taken from a high angle, either looking down on to heads, or sweeping across a line of faces pressed close to the front of the stage (thereby replicating the possible point of view of the band members) many shots were taken from a low angle looking up at the band. These shots aligned the position of the on-screen audience with the position of the viewer at home. The camera, therefore, was an intimate participant in the listening and playing of the 'live' musical experience. This intimacy is also supported by the fact that, aside from the shots of the crowd from the stage, there were otherwise very few long or establishing shots that would have exposed the *gap* between the stage and the crowd. When they were used, such shots tended to feature only at the beginning or the end of each performance thereby pulling the viewer into another item altogether. Used in this way, they were not a part of the music-image event itself, but acted as a signal that the viewer was about to be moved away from that specific performance frame.

In each item particular images did not therefore always follow each other in a way that followed any purely visual logic. Yet they were edited together in a way that referred either to the progress of the song—its rhythms, its climaxes—or to the apparent mood of the music. The fuzzy, slow motion video effects in The Happy Mondays' item, for example, were clearly related to the music's association with a drug infused frenzy of affect—as personified by Bez.

All of this, surprisingly, considering *Snub*'s avowed policy of producing a new way of looking at music and musical performance, actually demonstrate that the show continually reproduced a very conventional method of visualizing music on television. So much so that, as Andrew Goodwin has noted, for the habitual viewer of popular music on television, these conventions are 'so routine that they do not need specific illustration'. This should become obvious if we compare my analysis to Goodwin's summary of the conventional, visual arrangement of pop songs.

> The arrangement of pop songs balances three central elements: the voice, the rhythm, and the backing that supports them both. Broadly speaking, music video can be seen to mirror the prominence of the voice in pop by foregrounding the singer's face and (less centrally) emphasizing key rhythmic movements. Often there will be a tension in the cutting of images, between the emphasis on the pulse of the music and the imperative to return to the singer's face—a key anchoring moment, as Kaplan has noted. Most clips resolve this tension in favour of an emphasis on the latter . . . but there is usually some combination of rhythmic and vocal emphases. In this respect, as in many others, videos stress conventions already established in the lighting of rock concerts, where spotlights highlight singers and instrumentalists at key moments, and where lighting is used to create dramatic effects that punctuate the music in accord with its rhythm.[39]

Snub therefore replicates most, if not all, of the conventions that have come to be associated with music on television, and, as Goodwin is pointing out here, these have also been transferred to the music video. If *Snub* was so obviously conventional—particularly in its reproduction of the 'live'—how did the programme come, in the words of one enthusiastic American reviewer, to be described as an 'anti-show'? And why did this reviewer like it so much that he concludes his article by suggesting that, 'if it survives without selling out, something like it could be the American Bandstand of the future'?[40] The answer, as I have suggested, was partly due to the fact that the programme was

---

39 Andrew Goodwin, *Dancing in the Distraction Factory: Music, Television and Popular Culture* (Bloomington, Ind., and Minneapolis: University of Minnesota Press, 1992), 63–4.

40 C. Johnston, 'I Have Snubbed the Future', *Village Voice*, 20 Oct. 1987, 24.

careful to publicize its low budget and insider music credentials. But the success of the programme was also located in the *quality* rather than in the content or structure of the image, and by the way in which the visual element of the show was deliberately amateur and un(television)-professional. This is surprising, given that such amateurishness will be detrimental to the legibility image; after all, as the same reviewer observed:

> The first few shows, which aired in August, were scarred by poor audio, lousy editing, and shaking cameras.[41]

While the reviewer mentions such faults only to claim they have been reduced during the series run, I would argue that they were actually an important part of the show's success—a highly visible mark of the producers' creative amateurism. Such 'faults' provided evidence for Kelly and Fowler's stance as enthusiastic fans, rather than bored telly professionals. Brenda Kelly, for example, is quoted as saying that:

> Snub was just a crazy idea that we didn't think would happen because none of us had any money and I'd never made a TV programme before.[42]

Here, her professed amateurism is used to suggest that the programme offers something different from mainstream music television and from MTV. In contrast to these other forms of television, the videos and musical items that *Snub* produces and screens are presented as rough and ready and thus, crucially, authentic; *verité* documents rather than commercial packages. Another reviewer, for example, argued that:

> We're talking, lean scratched-together video, where big-buck production values *do not* try to make up for utterly banal talent behind.[43]

These comments are particularly revealing: they demonstrate a belief that *Snub*, whilst remaining conventional in terms of structure, differs in a qualitative sense from other representations of music on television. Primarily, this difference is established because the show *looked* cheap. This was true in all areas of the programme. During interviews, for example, the limitations imposed by the presence of only one or two cameras enabled few establishing shots or wider compositions; this created characteristically cramped and overcrowded images. In addition, the lack of resources and budget was also made

41 Ibid.

42 Brenda Kelly, quoted in M. Aston, 'TV for the Masses', *Underground* (Nov. 1987), 12.

43 Bill Raden, 'I Want my *Snub TV*', *Los Angeles Times*, 17 Oct. 1987, 16.

evident by the spartan qualities of many of the specially produced *Snub* videos, several of which were reminiscent of amateur filming practices. Characteristically, certain locations tend to predominate— empty beaches, back gardens, empty churches, and urban rooftops. As apparent amateurs these low budget professionals film in cheap, accessible places where permission to film was likely to be easy to obtain and free of charge.

In many ways, the programme's aesthetic foreshadowed another distinctive genre of television programming produced with the youth audience in mind. Later programmes produced by the BBC were also to employ a similar attitude and style. Related (but not necessarily tied) to the use and increasing prevalence of domestic camcorders it was a style that was developed in shows like *Takeover TV*, and was also adapted for a more serious documentary purpose in both the *The Living Soap* as well as in the junior version of the *Video Diaries* series, the *Teenage Diaries*. The camcorder style was distinguished by jerky, badly focused shots and often carried the marks of the technology of the video camera on to the final image, so that the date and time counter, and the frame designed to help amateur camera operators focus could often be seen on screen. *Snub* used such images for many of the same reasons that these later shows did; low production values were an on-screen reminder and guarantee of credibility.

While this amateur look was akin to the style of a magazine pro- gramme such as *Network 7*, *Snub*'s aesthetic additionally suggested a connection to the remnants of a Punk sensibility. The Punk ethos had notoriously established that 'anyone could start a band with three chords and guitar'. Because the videos and presentation of the pro- gramme were so amateur, *Snub*'s viewers could feel that 'anyone'— they—could be in a band and make a video that would be screened on the show.

Yet, ultimately, I suspect that it was more likely that it was not so much that 'anyone could do that'—that is, be on the show—but rather that only a few people would have the sophistication to appre- ciate it. The show's inclusion of its audience was not so much literal then, as implicit in its mode of address: *Snub*'s aesthetic was such that it required a specific cultural sensibility which would enable a par- ticular part of the audience to understand the programme's appeal. Importantly, this audience would actually be relatively exclusive in terms of what they liked and did not like; in the kind of cultural activities they would take part in; and were likely to be very particular —of course—about the kind of music they liked and would listen to. It is this audience that Christopher Johnston, for example, is describ- ing in his ironic comments on the 'normal people' who would want to watch the show, and their specific problems in coinciding with the show's late night scheduling in the United States.

> The drawback is that *Snub TV* airs at 1 a.m.—a time when normal
> people are out having fun. It's rebroadcast Sunday morning at
> 5 a.m. which is about the time normal people roll into bed.[44]

'Normal' people are, of course, young people who have got a social
life, and in Johnston's view they will therefore be those who are least
likely to be able to watch the show that is designed for them. Normal
people are therefore a very specific kind of people—young, with
active social lives who are also—probably—urban. In fact, the failure
to catch the programme, as Johnston is suggesting here, is almost an
indication that they are the appropriate audience. The answer to this
apparent paradox is, of course, to videotape the programme and in
the United States the producers were willing to send tape-sized liner
sleeves to facilitate this process. The opportunity to box and store the
show as if it were a collector's item—whether such an offer was taken
up or not—reveals another aspect of the show's putative relationship
to youth: its attempt to establish itself as a particular kind of cult viewing. The cult aspects of the show were also encouraged in Britain;
when the programme was shown in the UK it also appeared in a late
night slot.

Generally scheduled for a flexible 'approximately 11.30 p.m.' slot
this meant that the show was sometimes on later than advertised,
or abandoned when sports or other live shows overran. In terms of
its cult status such apparently careless scheduling was not necessarily unfortunate. Inadvertently, perhaps, the erratic appearance
of the show meant that the programme, apart from being hard to
look at, was also hard to find in the first place. Locating the programme required a particular kind of dedication and knowledge.
The programme establishes itself therefore as a cult; the cult insider is
distinguished by his or her possession of particular kinds of knowledge or habits that other individuals do not have. Thus, by being
aware of the show's existence, and by being someone who watches
television when most people do not, the *Snub* viewer is established
as a cult television viewer. This makes them conspicuously different
from the average television viewer, whose knowledge might be
limited—like everyone else in Britain—only to exactly what time and
day of the week that *Top of the Pops* is on. The cult status of the show
is also guaranteed by the low ratings figures for the show. Rather than
indicating the show's lack of popularity low audience figures actually
confirmed its credible, cutting edge status. It suggested that it was
watched by discriminating viewers, who themselves only watched
television when they had nothing better to do instead—like be in the
pub or at a gig.

44 Johnston, 'I Have Snubbed the Future'.

Snub's cultish inaccessibility was also closely and appropriately associated with the music selected for the programme. This was explicitly non-mainstream—though not just 'indie rock' as my description has perhaps overemphasized. Yet the show's likely minority appeal presented a potential problem for its producers. A minority audience—in this case a sub-audience within the already small youth audience—might not be justifiable within a mass medium like television. Interestingly, Peter Fowler responds to this worry by harking back to a version of the public service ethos espoused by John Reith.

> 'I don't accept that,' says Fowler. 'I think the fact that we're now getting an audience of one-million means that if you show something that's good, they'll grow to like it.'[45]

What Fowler is trying to claim here is akin to John Reith's requirement that television should 'lead' its audience's tastes rather than simply reflect them. Thus the programme's 'goodness', that is, literally, the 'showing of something good', is also established by the music. The music naturally reveals its essential worthiness through a process of a seemingly inevitable, and gradual, appreciation—much like the educational or acculturation process more commonly associated with the benefits of classical music. This evolutionary process is presumably what Fowler is implying when he says that the audience will 'grow to like it'. In doing this, he refers to something else that has a particular importance to the youth audience that may be watching, and this relates to the notion of essential 'goodness' in the music. For it is here that we can understand Fowler's position in relation to the argument outlined by Simon Frith earlier on in this chapter. Frith suggests that, at its most basic level, musical appreciation is always about aesthetics *and* ethics. Thus the 'goodness' or the credibility of *Snub* and the music it promotes not only speaks *to* (addresses) but also speaks *of* (articulates) the cultural sensibility of the audience. Frith, for instance, argues that:

> It is in deciding—playing and hearing what sounds *right*
> (I would extend this account of music from performing to
> listening, to listening as a way of performing)—that we both
> express ourselves, our own sense of rightness, and suborn
> ourselves, lose ourselves, in an act of participation.[46]

Snub has therefore orchestrated an aesthetic that champions a particular way of representing credibility, authenticity, and exclusivity. It produces a musical, televisual space where tastes are not simply

---

45 Quoted in Shearman, 'More Pop and Less Champagne'.

46 Frith, 'Music and Identity', 110.

reflected but *defined*. While the audience establishes its own credibility through watching the programme, the programme itself becomes
credible because of its dedicated audience of knowledgeable viewers.
This loop of mutual vindication is simply perhaps a more exclusive,
and, for dedicated audience members, ultimately a more *inclusive*,
version of Jody Berland's conception of a self-vindicating circle of
'semantic flattery'.

Learning how to appreciate music *in the right way* from *Snub*
implies sophistication, both in relation to the audience's developing
musical taste and more generally in their creation of a public identity.
So, although *Snub*'s tactic appears to escape the supposed contamina-
tion of the mediation effect—its rhetoric was about being 'anti-
television' and therefore pro-music—it too cannot ultimately break
free of a determining televisual structure which was based upon some
pretty familiar visual codes and conventions.

Yet not all youth music programmes produced during this time
period were concerned with credibility in this way. In a show like *The
Word* spartan, arty videos would not have integrated satisfactorily
with the programme's increasingly camp excess. Appearing on *The
Word*, however, was not a soft option for musical performers. Despite
the space given over to music, and despite the relative mix of musical
genres, the programme tended to feature the harder or heavier aspects
of the contemporary popular music scene such as hip-hop, rap, and
grunge. This editorial policy was determined not only by the fact that
bands appearing on the show might literally have to fight to establish
a place in the studio but, increasingly, the male or lad-ish bias of the
show in general.

This lad-ish attitude was to emerge strongly in the wider culture of
male youth in the 1990s; publications like the semi-pornographic
Loaded and the success of programmes like *Men Behaving Badly*
(a sit-com), *Fantasy Football League*, *They Think It's All Over* (a sport-
related chat and a sport-related quiz show), as well as *The White Room*
(a music show) and *Never Mind the Buzzcocks* (a pop quiz hosted
by Mark Lamarr) were all indicative of this new identity. The 'new lad'
(as opposed to the 'new man') had its origins in an article by Tony
Parsons, but it was also associated with the success of Nick Hornby's
best-selling 'autobiography' *Fever Pitch* (1992) (about the author's
obsession with the Arsenal football team) and, latterly, with the
same author's novel *High Fidelity* (1995) (which was predominantly
about a young man's obsession with his record collection and his
awkward relations with women). In general terms, the 'lad-ish attitude' might be summed up as a reflection of these programmes' and
publications' concerns, and the lad was popularly understood to be a
young heterosexual male who was obsessed with music and/or sport
(preferably football) but took nothing else seriously.

The rise of the lad and his particular affinity with certain kinds of music was and continues to be championed by Chris Evans in his music magazine show. While I will not spend too much time in this chapter focusing on Evans himself, his aggressive lad-ish pose, which can be seen in his performance of an apparently rampant hetero-sexuality, and in his reverence for football and footballing heroes, is also established by the way that music on his show establishes a particular kind of authenticity.

The space given up to music on *TFI Friday*, unlike *The Word*, is literal: based in the Riverside Studios, the programme is separated into two levels. On the ground level a wide area is occupied by a fixed hexagonal stage which juts out into a young, enthusiastic audience. One show begins (fairly typically) with Evans walking into this space from backstage. During his journey he passes through the crowd whom he occasionally acknowledges like a politician at a rally, or like a footballer coming on to the pitch. Reaching one corner of the stage, he stops to introduce the band; and literally 'hands over' his control of the show to the music, and directs the camera to the musical perform-ance that is about to take place. Once this is done, the studio director edits freely between a series of different cameras, some of which are on stage and some of which are both above and within the crowd. In effect, what Evans does in this sequence is to establish a place for him-self as part of the audience, thus relegating his own position to that of fan. It is an extremely conventional move—presenters do this on *Top of the Pops*—in a programme that otherwise demonstrably attempts to disrupt or subvert other televisual conventions.

The space for music is even more firmly established as different and special by the fact that the chat and comic items that feature in the programme are confined upstairs into the 'pub'. The pub includes a bar, a small group of invited guests, the film crew, and a battered desk that Evans uses as a base for interviews and links. The intimacy of the space is further emphasized by the way in which Evans is surrounded by suitably homely and lad-ish props. In the first series this included posters of Oasis and a cardboard figure of Pulp's Jarvis Cocker.

Since its inception the show has had two time slots in Channel 4's Friday night schedule; initially it was screened at 6 p.m. and at this time the music's authenticity was guaranteed by the fact that it was live: since the earliest days this has now become '*live*' rather than live. In an early interview with the free-minded Shaun Ryder, where he used 'fuck' amongst other swear words, the show became subject to a censor friendly ten-second or, reportedly, even longer thirty-minute delay. Yet the creation of the musical experience as being specifically authentic and immediate is still encouraged by the way in which the mayhem and cynicism upstairs is distanced from the musical per-formances downstairs.

There are instances in *TFI Friday*, however, where music is performed upstairs, but these are also moments where authenticity is foregrounded. In these instances Evans will interview a singer or musician—those favoured have included Mick Hucknall, Sting, and Noel Gallagher—and after a brief chat he will then challenge the performer to sing, or perform, there and then, 'live' and apparently unrehearsed, with perhaps a backing tape from a cassette recorder on the desk, or with a guitar Evans just happens to have to hand. With some persuasion most guests obligingly perform. While such instances might be expected, within the farcical, irreverent context of the show, to produce moments that are detrimental to the affect of the music and produce moments of karaoke-like embarrassment, they generally provide instances where the performers reveal their skills in their rawest sense. In these sequences the performer is revealed as a skilled individual. By framing the performer like this, as ordinary and as amateur, Evans effectively recasts the celebrity interviewee as a craftsman, who is honest because he (rarely she) is vulnerable. From this position performers are able to demonstrate that they can really sing or play without the protection or support of extensive studio production, and thus that they are actually who they claim to be—a singer, songwriter, or musician. This therefore suggests that they are authentic at the most basic level. In addition, such moments are often heightened by the fact that these sequences are often particularly privileged, partly by the fact that the pub is actually quiet during the performance, and partly by the fact that they are often repeated later on in the show, or appear again in later weeks. These moments also provide an opportunity for the performer to acknowledge the pub's generally enthusiastic response in a very personal and intimate way—by nodding, or glancing shyly at Chris and the crowd, or by a certain amount of disingenuous self-deprecation. Obviously all of this represents a relationship that the viewer is also able, vicariously, to enter into. These sequences appear authentic because they bring the viewer in, closer to the performer. As part of the in-crowd in the pub, viewers at home may feel that they are witness to a breakdown in the boundaries between themselves and the creator or source of the music. With the negation of distance, they are then able to feel—because they believe that they can see—the process of music making itself and it is this which guarantees authenticity. The exception to this unsurprisingly occurs when Evans interviews singers who are more obviously commercial and who are, therefore, potentially inauthentic. Kylie Minogue, for example, was not asked to sing live but teased by Evans into recalling the lyrics of her infamous and seriously un-hip 1980s hit 'I Should Be So Lucky' which was in clear contradistinction to her new and aspirationally hipper image and musical style.

Most of the music performed on the show is organized spatially in a way that lends it authority and which validates a particular kind of authenticity. As I have suggested it is an authenticity where the aura of the music is putatively inscribed on its television performance by the way that it is arranged visually, and in the way in which it lays claim to the 'live' and, at different times, to the presence of musicianship and skill. The relationship between musicianship, 'liveness', and skill is also replicated in the authenticity constructed in another current music show, *Later . . . with Jools Holland. Later . . .*'s similarity to *TFI Friday* can be seen in the way that the music's affect is inversely related to the apparent space given to the musicians. In *Later . . .* (and in *TFI Friday*) musical affect is represented and authenticated because the studio appears cavernous and the musicians have the space to surround themselves with the paraphernalia of live musical performance —amps, wires, and bottles of water. This is in sharp contrast to a show like *Live and Kicking* where performers are obliged to integrate themselves into a small area of a set designed for other purposes. Understandably, various musicians' attempts to integrate themselves into such programmes are not always successful, and they can end up looking slightly ridiculous. This misfit between environment, performer, and the audience was a common occurrence on another Saturday morning children's show—*What's Up Doc?*—which had a cartoon theme, featuring, at one time, a kind of primary coloured jungle backdrop including fake polystyrene boulders. This led to a diverse selection of musicians performing uncomfortably, all too conscious of the discrepancy between the musical affect they were trying to achieve and the artificial location they were obliged to perform within. The discrepancy between the kinds of authenticity constructed by shows such as *Live and Kicking* and *Later . . .* is not countered by the fact that different bands appear on each show, as, in fact, both programmes can and do feature the same artists: Pulp, for example, appeared on both *Later . . .* and *Live and Kicking* while East 17 have also appeared on both *TFI Friday* and *What's Up Doc?*

The musical performers who seem most at ease in these difficult television environments are, unsurprisingly, those performers who are associated with a genre of music where affect is not dominated by the need to reproduce a particular kind of credibility associated with the representation of 'liveness' or musicianship. Instead, for these groups, the presence and exuberance of the performers themselves generate affect. Supported by lively dance moves and stylish costumes this is a strategy that has been used by many musical groups, most notably by Motown groups such as The Supremes or The Jackson Five. It also has its origins in television variety shows, end of the pier cabarets, and the Hollywood musical. In the late 1980s and early 1990s, boy bands, following in these footsteps, also relied on this kind of showmanship to embody the energy and youthfulness of the music. Of the groups that emerged during this period Take That's appearances on *Going Live* (the previous incarnation of *Live and Kicking*) demonstrated how music continued to be successfully articulated through television by a concentration of the affectual power of the music on to the bodies of the performers. In these music-image sequences, bodies became the focus because the conventional musicians' props (guitars, drums, and microphones) which indicate where the music originates from were rarely used. Indeed, guitars or other instruments only appeared when the song was a ballad—for example, in one of Take That's Christmas hits, 'Babe', a grand piano and a guitar were 'played' by two group members in their numerous promotional television appearances. These musical props appeared because dancing—by the boys or the on-screen audience—was not feasible. In contrast to this, during a dance track—such as, for example, 'Could it be Magic'—the lack of focus in the musical per-formances was compensated for by the fact that much of the image-music event was occupied by the display of carefully choreographed dance routines, and fast editing on the beat, revealing and integrat-ing supposedly spontaneous moments that demonstrated different group members' trademark gestures. These might include Robbie's 'cheeky grin' and floppy fringe, or Mark's bare midriff and dolphin tattoo. Take That along with other boy bands before and after—from New Kids on the Block to Boyzone—are entertainers in the broadest sense, and they are therefore pin-ups and television celebrities as well as musicians. The mutual dependence of Take That with the teenage music magazine *Smash Hits* emphasized this aspect. Notoriously, for example, *Smash Hits* featured Take That on its front cover before they had a single in the charts. The purely voyeuristic pleasure Take That encouraged must have allowed for a subordination of musical affect for at least some of their fans, and in this instance the band's actions functioned simply as an advertisement for the consumption of images and other non-musical commodities such as magazines, posters, and T-shirts. In addition, various cross-promotional activities, such as Take That presenting Channel 4's *The Big Breakfast* for a week, and their diverse merchandizing—including jewellery and their reproduction as dolls—functioned comfortably within the increas-ingly self-reflexive and media heavy public sphere; a world further endorsed by programmes such as *Going Live* and *Live and Kicking*. Importantly, the band's ability to diversify was not seen by their fans as 'selling out' but as increasing their accessibility and as part of a self-conscious knowingness about the band's character. One indication of this knowing irony was the cover of Take That's Greatest Hits album which showed a kitsch shrine filled with different TT paraphernalia but giving pride of place to the dolls of the band members.

Music making and music listening in this context was a very different activity from the kind of music celebrated and validated by programmes such as *Snub*; however, the specific qualities of music as a form of expression were still important. In part, this is because the success of each performance of a band like Take That relies on music's unique ability simultaneously to address the individual, while also establishing a community, and to do so in a way that is not, as in television's non-musical direct address, purely imaginary, or transient. As part of the boy band experience the musical aspect was crucial because music, unlike the poster on the bedroom wall, or the television appearance, could be transported and more importantly replayed: in headphones, on CD players, or in loud choruses at the back of the bus. These different forms of musical transference meant that the associations generated by the performance—of fun, togetherness, love, and even 'youthfulness'—could also be resituated. Indeed, while *Smash Hits* reproduces images it also prints the lyrics of the songs, which, while not quite akin to the publication of music and lyric sheets earlier in the twentieth century, does mean that a certain kind of amateur performance is still being encouraged, even if this is simply a giggly, communal sing-along. For this musical audience, therefore, musical affect was generated in a more functional way, creating a space for certain pleasures whether this was screaming your lungs out, singing the songs, or dancing the dances. Above all music saturated, and energized the personalities that performed. While this does, in part, imply that what was most valued was the visual—the cute outfits, the 'six pack' stomachs—this value was established by musical characteristics such as a perceptible and excessive sensuality, and a kind of responsiveness where affect was reinforced and narrativized during the musical performance.

The music event in these instances demanded a response because of the frequent repetition of words and melody within the song structure. The expectation or knowledge of such repetition meant that the viewer could and would expect the singer to smile, to look into the camera, or to frown at predictable moments during every television performance. It is therefore because of the music that the viewer who is also a listener is continually and often unavoidably cued into a direct and fantastic relationship with the performer. With Take That, as with other similar bands, such expectations were encouraged because the songs are often already familiar to the listener, either because they are covers of old songs, or because, simply, they have a predictable rhythm. The resonance of the 'already said' becomes in these instances empowering rather than disenchanting. Believing or realizing that you know what is going to happen next has its own kind of real pleasure and carries its own magic. Related activities such as the constant replaying of one song, the feeling of being 'in the groove' on the dance floor, all suggest that this kind of sensation is very powerful and creates an affect that is different but akin to the aura sought in other kinds of musical experience. In these situations the relationship between the viewer/listener and the music and the performer has a temporal as well as a spatial dimension. For each individual it will have qualities that are both generative ('I am making this happen—I am part of this') as well as speculative ('I am seeing this happen'). In other words, the viewer as listener responds to a temporal cue from the music and expects or knows that the singer will look at or address them *because* of the music. As the television image responds to this expectation it satisfies the listener as viewer, and obligingly fills the space of the screen with the expected close up of the face or the midriff just when the viewer knows, or is willing, the screen to be so filled.

So although the music seems tantalizingly close to being squeezed out of the picture it still provides a way of celebrating and validating personal and collective activities and identities. This kind of music also allows for and generates a space for young people's feelings and hopes, and, ultimately, their identities as sexual individuals, and the 1980s and 1990s boy bands, with their sculpted bodies and provocative poses made this very clear. Significantly, the teenager's sexual identity was no longer entirely confined within the boundaries of a clear-cut heterosexual identity. Take That's early public appearances at gay clubs and their androgynous appeal meant that they had a strong core of openly gay young fans, while the pretty boy/girl look of two of the band members—Mark Owen and Robbie Williams—encouraged rumours about their and the other band members' sexual orientation. Of course, the majority of Take That's fans were female, but they were more open about the sexual aspects of their fantastic relationship with the band than previous generations of screaming teens. This sexualization was undoubtedly encouraged by the visibility and explicit nature of teenage magazines that were popular in the early 1990s—notably *Sky* and *More!*—which were far more up front about sex—and specifically the pleasures of sex—than an earlier teen magazine such as *Jackie* would ever have been. *More!* for example (a magazine aimed at 13–17-year-old girls) carries a feature called 'position of the fortnight' showing sketched figures demonstrating a variety of different sexual poses. In relation to Take That the content of banners waved at the band during their concert appearances—such as 'Fuck me Robbie!'—also indicated that a new pose of aggressive female sexuality was being taken up by teenage girls who were openly sexually knowledgeable even though they were not necessarily sexually active. Music might therefore be said to have been an excuse, but it also offered legitimate ways for fans to respond to and repeat important experiences and emotions. The web of fantasy orchestrated through the display of bodies, by the constant repetition of direct address, and in the way that each old or new song repackaged strong emotions on to familiar faces and located them within one place, demonstrated the power and authentic reach of the music.

The young television viewer in the late 1980s and 1990s, therefore, continued to watch as television attempted to produce convincing image-music sequences in a variety of ways. The differences between performances and formats can be seen to relate to the importance given to various kinds of authenticity by each programme's producers, and, as I have shown, these versions of what can be understood to be authentic are clearly an attempt to articulate, on the behalf of particular audiences, a series of self-validating conceptions of what 'authenticity' is. This means that musical performances are often spaces within programmes that remain open to a sincere investment by the viewer even when elsewhere the programme is openly cynical or reflexive about the mechanisms of fame and celebrity. However, this is an investment that was subject to, and arranged in accordance with, the very particular demands of individuals or smaller groups of viewers, who were implicated in the justification and appreciation of specific forms of musical pleasure.

The intense and necessary fragmentation of the musical audience explains many instances of the misfit between image and sound, as viewers who are listeners refused to buy in to visual conventions that they saw as inappropriate or clumsy. It also explains how a minority show like *Snub* could be deemed to be as successful as a mainstream programme such as *Going Live*. In the post-1960s, post-modern music scene it was no longer easy to identify comfortably with images and sounds that were acknowledged to be always already commercial. Yet, rather than closing down the options for music on television, what this tension encouraged was the emergence of many other different and increasingly diverse places for music on television and in other visual media.

The generation who negotiated such an expanding territory were persuaded, enthralled, and absorbed by music, but were also no longer obliged to align their emotions to the contours of the traditional studio-based youth music programme as it attempted to usurp, or provide an escape from, the domestic environment. In fact, with the increasing use of visual media outside the family living room (in bedrooms) as well as outside the home (in clubs and pubs) there was a need for visual representations which could integrate with, rather than dominate, the environment and imagination of the young viewer. The increasing televisualization of festivals and concerts both on site—by the use of large video screens at festivals and gigs—and in the festivals' own appearances in the television schedules (inspired by the success of Live Aid in 1985 and followed by extended coverage of

Glastonbury and other festivals) illustrated a shift in the geography of youth, music, and television. 'Zoo TV', U2's mammoth project/tour in the early 1990s, was also a response to this, and in its use of massive banks of video screens, hand-held cameras, and the creation of its own TV channel it parodied and celebrated the increasingly technological and mediatized aspects of live performance. The social and technological effect of small and big media—whether it was the portable television in the bedroom, the Sony Walkman and camcorder, or MTV and Diamondvision stadium replays—irrevocably changed the way in which images and music impacted on one another and how, inevitably, television could and would take part in this process. While U2 flashed 'Watch More TV' on huge video banks they sang live to the converted who, like the band, had often travelled miles to be there—in the flesh. Alternatively, in the heady days of the early rave scene, young people travelled to arrive in the middle of nowhere, to dance to digitally orchestrated snatches of music and sound that had already been heard and felt many times before. Roving under the light of video screens they might respond to, but not really see, digitized visual representations of the beat, or glimpse snatches of old television programmes. Ultimately, of course, they could sometimes have seen themselves—live and 'live'—caught on camera, dancing.

4

'You Can Take It From Me That What I Say Is Absolutely Gospel' Game Shows and Generation X

GAME shows or television quizzes are regarded by many critics as the 'trashiest' form of television programming. Garry Whannel, for instance, has claimed that:

> With the exception of the intellectual quizzes (*Mastermind*, *University Challenge*, and so on) few televisual forms have as low a cultural status as quiz shows. They are regularly derided by middle-class opinion, criticized in government reports, and restricted in quantity and value of prizes by the IBA.[1]

However, they are also, as he goes on to say, both cheap to make and popular with audiences (at least in terms of ratings.) It is not surprising therefore that many game shows are aimed at, and appeal to, younger generations of television viewers. In this chapter I will look at two examples of this pervasive television genre and use them to demonstrate how the game show genre was adapted for Generation X. I will discuss two very distinctive programmes, the *Crystal Maze* and *Gamesmaster*, vivid examples that illustrate certain characteristics, such as exaggeration, camp, irreverence, reflexivity, and a 'trash' or post-modern aesthetics, which are symptomatic of the version of youth television I have been describing. While there has not been a great deal of critical discussion concerning game shows (despite their prevalence in television schedules), most academic analyses have been concerned to demonstrate how the programmes establish a

---

1 Garry Whannel, 'Winner Takes All: Competition', in A. Goodwin and G. Whannel (eds.), *Understanding Television* (London and New York: Routledge, 1990), 104. This rule has obviously been relaxed by the ITC—the inception and massive success of *Who Wants to be a Millionaire?* is one programme self-evidently not restricted in the value of the prizes it can award.

logic for the accelerating 'commodity culture' of Western capitalism. It is argued (with slightly different inflections by critics such as Garry Whannel, John Fiske, and Bill Lewis for example) that this 'logic' is articulated through the valorization of particular kinds of knowledge—and this is knowledge that is either 'factual' (academic and empirical) or 'human' (social and interpersonal). In each show, they argue, it is the appropriate exhibition of such knowledges which allows contestants, who are both spectators and participants, to progress (with a certain amount of luck) in order to 'win', whether it be prizes or esteem. These journeys, it is suggested, are always ideological, in that they allow certain ideologies to emerge as inevitable by-products of the game-as-ritual. The 'norms' of behaviour that are celebrated and established by the game and the host appear to be inevitable because they are aligned to a spatial hierarchy, which defines who stands where, who gets to move, and who gets to speak. This hierarchy is organized and dictated by the structure and setting of the studio as well as the rules of the actual game. Bill Lewis, for example, claims:

> The physical positioning of spectator/participant within
> various game show spaces indicates elements of control
> within hierarchical structures. Thus the spectator/participant
> acknowledges homage to the perceived importance of the event
> by dressing formally. Further, a common icon of these games is
> the desk behind which s/he sits or stands in the game's initial
> stages. The successful player gains the right to move from the desk
> to another playing space and with it the right to play for greater
> rewards. This sign of success reinforces complex and powerful
> myths of social and educational mobility.[2]

Here, then, 'complex and powerful myths' are choreographed within the rigid confines of the studio set; social mobility and the power to consume are materialized into a spatial progression as the successful contestant exhibits the appropriate form of knowledge enabling them literally to move (or be moved) around the studio. Even when shows are not based around the acquisition of desirable consumer goods or on the exhibition of particularly legitimate forms of knowledge, spatial progress is always linked with success, as Whannel explains in relation to the celebrity game show, *Blankety Blank*:

> Contestants do not walk on; the elaborate machinery of the set
> wheels them on, and if they lose, it wheels them off again. To win
> through the early stages is to win the right of movement—you
> get to stand up and be pushed into position by Les Dawson. In

2 Bill Lewis, 'TV Games: People as Performers', in L. Masterman (ed.), *TV Mythologies* (London: Comedia/Routledge, 1984), 43.

achieving final victory, as well as the self-consciously 'cheap' prizes, you win entry into the world of celebrities: the winner is taken over to meet the panel.[3]

Whannel thus implies that while the show may not subscribe to the lure of commodity fetishism by showering contestants with expensive prizes, the programme does offer an equally transitory and dubious opportunity: the possibility of a brief 'transportation' into the world of glamour and celebrity.

John Fiske also constructs his discussion of game and quiz shows along similar lines to both Whannel and Lewis, although, characteristically, he is keen to retain some sense in which game show viewers (unlike contestants) are 'not necessarily incorporated into the consumerist ideology'.[4] Nevertheless, even he admits that:

> Quiz shows, like advertising, are undoubtedly part of commodity capitalism, and use many of the similar cultural strategies. For instance, glamorous models are used to display the prizes and thus associate commodities with sexuality, thereby linking buying with sexual desire and satisfaction.[5]

While the 'entertaining' aspects of the shows are often played down in such discussions, both Fiske and Whannel do suggest that the conventional excess of the programmes, such as the excessive display of emotion, the garish sets, the rapid editing and voyeuristic display of consumer goods, means that the programmes offer a glimpse of a possibly subversive, carnivalesque, or utopian community which may draw in viewers in a positive way. Whannel explains:

> Richard Dyer suggests that popular entertainment characteristically offers abundance, energy, and community, in contrast to the scarcity, exhaustion, and isolation more common to lived reality. He argues that entertainment is in this sense often rooted in a utopian sensibility, offering an idealized world from which scarcity, tiredness, and loneliness have been eliminated. While it is in no sense utopian, a show like *The Price is Right* could be seen in these terms, for it is nothing if not exuberant. Everything about the staging of the show is designed to produce the impression of energy and the audience are galvanised into a temporary frenetic community.[6]

From these perspectives we can see that game shows can be argued to offer a variety of characteristic enticements to the television viewer:

3 Ibid., 106. The show is now hosted by the drag artist Lily Savage.
4 John Fiske, in *Television Culture* (London: Routledge, 1987), 273.
5 Ibid., 272.
6 Whannel, 'Winner Takes All', 107.

(i)   the valorization of particular kinds of knowledge (but only so far as it can be used in a way that is discrete and appropriate),

(ii) the lure of seductive commodities as markers of social (as spatial) progress,

(iii) a frenetic, possibly utopian, sensibility and/or community,

(iv) the simultaneous establishment of, and temporary access to, a world of glamour and celebrity.

For the young audience that grew up in the 1980s in Britain, the game show's various and characteristic enticements were particularly relevant and seductive. Living in a period marked by an increasing fragmentation of society, and thus perhaps an increasing anxiety about 'belonging' the communal aspects of the game show were appealing. In addition, magazines and other television programmes continued to encourage a desire for both commodities and fame. Finally, living in the post-modern moment, Generation X was also privy to a growing awareness that established (or doctrinal) forms of knowledge were increasingly open to question. It is interesting to note that the two game shows I will discuss seem to have effectively tapped into some wider aspects of British popular culture, as their television success resulted in lucrative spin-offs for their creators; whether this is in the form of mini-theme parks and books (the *Crystal Maze*), or theme days and a magazine (the *Gamesmaster*). Similarly, it is not surprising that one of the shows exists, in part, as a direct advertisement for a particular product and culture—the computer game and computer game culture (the *Gamesmaster*). This direct involvement of the game show outwith the television medium confirms the increasing horizontal integration of related media forms, but it also illustrates that these shows are no longer simply idealized, or aspirational rituals that are necessarily separate from, or opposed to, the viewer's reality—as Dyer's analysis suggests. The success of these various spin-offs demonstrates the ease with which these shows are able to capitalize on their distinctive and coherent aesthetic strategies. This, crucially, allows them not only to promote consumption, but also to be bought effectively as if they were material commodities in their own right.

While these wider cultural tendencies indicate that this genre has a particular resonance for this audience, at the same time the adherence of conventional game shows to the validation of traditional forms of knowledge, and to particular forms of desire, as well as a successful reproduction of a 'utopian vision' of commodity culture, became increasingly problematic. These problems are exacerbated by the fact that the audience for the new game shows was resistant to, and overfamiliar with, the style, rubric, and ideologies associated with this genre of programming. This is both because these viewers were familiar with television, but also because, as young people, they may also have been students or, at least, recent products of an increasingly exam-oriented education system. As a group they would have a particular anathema towards projects which continued to validate pseudo-examinations that apparently served to legitimate certain kinds of knowledge or learning.

How, then, do the two shows I will discuss here try to provide answers to these problems? The answer is tied into the distinctive aesthetic strategy that links the two programmes. This strategy reproduces a distinctive and cohesive aesthetic that is characterized by a visual style and a moral ambivalence that could be claimed as recognizably post-modern. In their content the shows also celebrate a form of knowledge that might best be understood as 'dirty', 'fuzzy', and partial. Another aspect which links the programmes is the similarity of address, performance, and the (apparent) personality of the hosts who, I argue, demonstrate a peculiar form of 'sincere cynicism' in their articulation of, and relationship to, their role within each programme.

Both programmes produced a *mise en scène* that employed a florid extravagance, an excess of detail, and a kind of grotesque façade. In different ways each show embraced an aesthetic akin to the kind of architectural design of recent films such as *BladeRunner* (1982) and the *Alien* trilogy (1979; 1986; 1992). These films, along with the more predominantly 'neo-gothic' look of the recent *Batman* films (1989; 1992; 1995) (and their related graphic novels), are argued to be post-modern in design and character because they display a variety of styles—baroque, gothic, industrial, modern, and medieval, amongst others—as an overblown pastiche. In addition an atmosphere of accelerated decay and a morbid climate will often match this eclectic excess. In her article 'Ramble City: Postmodernism and *BladeRunner*' Guiliana Bruno provides a particularly useful analysis of this style:

> In *BladeRunner*, the visions of postindustrial decay are set in an inclusive, hybrid architectural design. The city is called Los Angeles, but it is an LA that looks very much like New York, Hong Kong, or Tokyo. We are not presented with a real geography, but an imaginary one: a real synthesis of mental architectures, of topoi. Quoting from different real cities, postcards, advertising, movies, the text makes a point about the city of postindustrialism. It is a polyvalent, interchangeable structure, the product of geographical displacements and condensations.[7]

Here, and in the rest of her article, Bruno describes how *BladeRunner* literally inscribes a post-modern *mise en scène* as the set informs the

---

7 Guiliana Bruno, 'Ramble City: Postmodernism and *BladeRunner*', in A. Kuhn (ed.), *Alien Zone: Cultural Theory and Contemporary Science Fiction Cinema* (London: Verso, 1990), 186.

narrative and articulates the post-modern concerns of the plot. Similarly, in his discussion concerning the first of the recent trilogy of *Batman* films, Jim Collins observes how the *mise en scène* is an active and vital part of an overarching post-modern sensibility that imbues the film:

> The narration of the film, the very formation of the *mise en scène*, depends upon a process of calling up the Gothic, but it also 'steals' specific shots from classical Hollywood films just as self-consciously. The high angle shots of the seemingly endless flights of stairs is reminiscent of *Vertigo* . . . and the alternation of high angle and low angle shots between the Joker and Batman and Vicky Vale as they hang from the side of the Cathedral is explicitly taken from the conclusion of *North by North-west* (as well as the climatic confrontation scene in *Blade Runner*). The invocation of texts as different as *Dracula*, Notre Dame de Paris, the Sagrada Familia, and *Vertigo*, as well as all the antecedent comic and graphic novel versions of Batman produces an eclecticism that is in many ways even more complicated than Gaudi's Cathedral, which Post-Modernist architects consider one of the high temples of eclecticism.[8]

In these films, the *mise en scène*, although by definition eclectic, also emerges as a recognizable aesthetic that results from, and in part defines, a sensibility or mood that articulates a form of 'post-industrial glamour' and sleaze.

Structurally, this may be understood to be post-modern because the design and architectural references that are taken up are used without reference to their specific histories and are combined in ways that have no respect to their differing cultural status. Bruno quotes Charles Jencks, who suggests what the effect of such an aesthetic might be:

> The resultant hybrid balances and reconciles opposed meanings . . . This inclusive architecture absorbs conflicting codes in an attempt to create (what Robert Venturi calls) 'the difficult whole' . . . It can include ugliness, decay, banality, austerity . . . In general terms it can be described as radical eclecticism or adhocism. Various parts, styles or sub-systems are used to create a new synthesis.[9]

The 'new synthesis' in the various media I have been referring to allows for a diversity of characters, narratives, and technologies to

8 Jim Collins, 'Batman: The Movie, Narrative: The Hyperconscious', in R. Pearson and W. Urrichio (eds.), *The Many Lives of Batman: Critical Approaches to a Superhero and his Media* (London: British Film Institute, 1991), 169.

9 Charles Jencks, quoted in Bruno, 'Ramble City', 186–7.

coalesce into a fluid, but coherent aesthetic. Mysterious figures—super-heroes, villains, magicians, and scientists—adventures, biographies, and myths, as well as old and new technologies, such as computers, cars, film, video, and photography, are all integrated into a *mise en scène* which creates a fantastic world out of industrial decay, and futuristic and fantastic architecture. This aesthetic, therefore, is semiotically rich, but as a pastiche it is also a patchwork of simulations, and its glamour and gloss stems in part from the fact that it is not real, but 'fantastically' real. As Bruno explains, citing Jean Baudrillard, it acts a form of 'hallucinatory resemblance'.[10] From this perspective, the real is argued no longer to exist, except as a kind of coded nostalgic simulation, that is here filtered through an aesthetic that has a dream-like, even nightmarish, quality.

It is not coincidental that this aesthetic has close links to the look and feel of many computer games. Julian Stallabrass, for example, in his article, 'Just Gaming: Allegory and Economy in Computer Games', provides another description that is akin to the aesthetic I am attempting to outline here:

> There is something familiar about the visual aspects of many games, and while this is partly because we already know their elements from films, cartoons, adverts and comics, beyond this they possess a crisp, hallucinatory clarity, the images being constructed from a precise repetition of tiny blocks of which the viewer may become aware. They exhibit a phantom objectivity, a hollowness, being a purer distillation of the generalized forms found in the commodity and the advertisement. To compensate for this lifeless immateriality, there frequently appear glowing objects, flashes, explosions, phantom lights, iridescence in which the ghostliness of the medium simulates an aura.[11]

This demonstrates again that this aesthetic can be understood to be characterized by the mix and dependent interrelationship of media —cartoons, films, advertisements—as well as a sense in which the scene produced is also, or appears to be, an hallucination, at times iridescent and fantastic. As Stallabrass also goes on to observe, many of the games also combine the material of science fiction with medieval architecture, or they may take the form of a 'Tolkienesque' fantasy mixed with modern-day weapons; so like *BladeRunner* they can be seen to collapse various 'exotic' cultures into an eclectic display. In addition to this, in many of the games the 'labyrinth' features heavily, whether it is as the dank interconnecting chambers of a dungeon—as

10 Ibid., 188.

11 Julian Stallabrass, 'Just Gaming: Allegory and Economy in Computer Games', *New Left Review*, 198 (1993), 86.

in a 'Sword and Sorcery' epic—or as a network of 'super-industrial' tunnels in a spaceship—as in *Alien*.

The computer game's close association with the aesthetic that I have been identifying can also be seen in this description of the successful game, 'Tomb Raider' (Core Design), written by Charlie Brooker for the computer game magazine PC Zone.

> 'Tomb Raider' concerns the exploits of one Lara Cruz (or Lara
> Croft—Core don't seem to have decided which yet)—a sort of a
> female Indiana Jones. Which isn't to say she's got a large chest and
> a stubbly chin—she does have big tits, but the stubble doesn't get
> a look in. The promotional artwork makes her look remarkably
> like Jamie Hewlett's *Tank Girl*—long legs, two guns and a sneer—
> while in the game itself she's somewhat reminiscent of Michelle
> from the 'Tekken' series . . . The plot has something to do with
> a thing called 'The Scion' which—in the finest videogame
> tradition—has been split into four parts and scattered around
> the world. And it hasn't been scattered anywhere safe or 'nice', like
> Center Parcs or Kew Gardens and the like. No no no, that would
> make a far more sensible, but infinitely duller game. The pieces
> have ended up in a bunch of dank and scary tombs, and it's your
> job to go and get them back.[12]

In this brief description, it is possible to see elements of the aesthetic that Stallabrass identifies; firstly, the interconnection between media; the allusion to film (Indiana Jones, and specifically *Raiders of the Lost Ark*); comics (*Tank Girl*—also an ill-fated film); and secondly, the notion of a quest. Finally, the *mise en scène* is also appropriate—the 'dank and scary tombs', which, as Brooker later notes, just happen to have 'an entire arsenal of fearsome weaponry scattered around in there'.[13] And this, too, is a fitting mix of modern and primitive technology, including blow-darts, fireballs, handguns, automatic shotguns, and iron spikes. Interestingly, much is also made of the fact that the game is a 'gorgeous' simulation, where backdrops have been laboriously layered to create an effect of three-dimensionality.

> What I'm trying to say is that it looks absolutely gorgeous. Cast
> your eyes over the screenshots and you'll no doubt hear yourself
> thinking something along the lines of 'hmm . . . looks just like
> 'Alone in the Dark' to me'. And you'd be more or less right. Until
> that is you see it in action. Which is when you realise that, unlike
> AITD games, 'Tomb Raider' is 'properly' three-dimensional.
> Those detailed backdrops aren't backdrops—they're constructed
> from fully interactive 3D objects.[14]

12 Charlie Brooker, 'Tomb Raider', *PC Zone*, 44 (Nov. 1996), 49.

13 Ibid., 49.

14 Ibid., 48–9.

The computer game is described here as an embracing simulation, where although the screen remains stubbornly two dimensional, the effect is three dimensional as the player moves through the labyrinth of tombs. There is a depth to the screen and a bizarre sense in which the ghastly—the tombs, monsters, the dank, and the dark—has become 'gorgeous', luminescent, and seductive. Stallabrass explains:

> Colours are bright and synthetic, the shapes they describe are predominantly geometrical, and become more so as they are resolved into polygonal surfaces or the differentiated squares of bit-mapped images. Yet games also play on the precise opposite of this glossy sci-fi world, particularly in the numerous dungeon scenarios where spaces appear dark, often damp, irregular and confining.[15]

The 'glossy sci-fi world' envisaged by many early science-fiction movies has been replaced by a stickier, danker, and darker territory, akin to the city visualized in *BladeRunner*, which as Bruno claims:

> is not ultramodern, but the post-modern city. It is not an orderly layout of skyscrapers and ultracomfortable, hypermechanized interiors. Rather, it creates an aesthetic of decay, exposing the dark side of technology, the process of disintegration.[16]

This post-modern aesthetic dresses a world where technology is futuristic but also messy and wasteful, and while it mixes historical periods and styles it has no apparent history of its own. In addition to this, different quotations of specific architectural styles (Egyptian, medieval, gothic) may, in some instances, be separated into specific quarters, or zones, that are similar only in the way that they can be distinguished by an eerily super-real, or hallucinatory quality.

Unsurprisingly, *Gamesmaster*, as a series that features different computer games, is much indebted to this kind of aesthetic. The first obvious indicator of this is that *Gamesmaster*, like many game shows, creates a 'fake' place. In the first few series, this place was a post-industrial 'resort' situated on an oil rig in the middle of a sea— seemingly somewhere, and potentially anywhere, it appeared to be the North Sea. Significantly, this meant that while the set itself was material (and I will describe this later), the location was virtual. The programme's opening titles begin as the television screen is 'scrambled' by a series of 'white noise' graphics which then settle into a simulation of a helicopter approaching the central landing pad of the rig. While the graphics vary in density and colour the predominant visual gloss is achieved by the colouring of skeletal, architectural, 'blueprints' of the rig and helicopter that are viewed throughout the

15 Stallabrass, 'Just Gaming', 86.
16 Bruno, 'Ramble City', 185.

sequence from a series of different angles. Various 'shots' are edited together throughout this sequence, some from below, some beside, and others within the helicopter itself. As the graphics increase in size and density, they work to pull the viewer into the ultimate destination of the rig. This functions very much as a series of more conventional close-ups might have done, although there is a sense that the objects appear, as in the 'Tomb Raider' game, to be 'fully interactive 3D objects'. The sequence ends with the emergence of the Gamesmaster (played by Patrick Moore, hitherto best known as the presenter of the long running BBC astronomy series *The Sky at Night*) who appears to be digitized and is thereby integrated into this virtual place, as his face flickers into vision underneath a chrome helmet that makes up part of the rig itself.

Patrick Moore's performance as the Gamesmaster is significant, since his contribution is an ironic homage to the old school notion of 'big' science of the 1950s, 1960s, and 1970s—big telescopes, moon landings, and meteors. This provides a distinct contrast to the new school of science characterized by 'soft' technology that is small, compact, and often portable such as computer games, the Walkman, and nano-technology. Moore's re-presentation as a supposed expert and controller of the games and tasks is intentionally ironic. Although as 'Chrome Dome' (as he is sometimes called) he seems to take his incorporation in good part, there is also a sense in which any authority that he might have had through his association with previous legitimate forms of knowledge—such as the mysteries of the galaxy and other difficult information that needed explaining to the layman —is being ridiculed. In the context of the show this legitimate knowledge is superseded by the kinds of knowledge validated by the programme, such as prices and manufacturers, which games are worth playing, individual game playing skills, and advice on how to cheat. The patronizing tones and other-worldly demeanour of many old school popular science presenters—such as James Burke, Jonathan Miller, Magnus Pyke, even David Attenborough—are thereby digitally re-mastered and parodied. Such references are, however, possibly lost on the current generation of viewers, many of whom were probably born some years after the ultimate triumph of big science—the moon landing. Nevertheless, Moore's presence is a deliberate and ironic allusion to previous popular science programmes and adds an element of knowingness to the skeleton of the virtual, fake place.

In contrast to the virtual location of the programme, the *Gamesmaster* set (in the original 1992 series) emphasizes its material nature. Once inside, at the beginning of each programme, the camera swoops down through a confusion of heavy, gloomy architecture. This consists of several metal stairways, various interconnecting levels and balconies, as well as an abundance of superfluous, clunky, and redundant technology—including fake instrument panels with large old-fashioned dials and levers, and 'miles' of metal tubing covering the walls. This creates a spectacular sense of depth which is enhanced by the positioning of the audience on several levels, who peer over the balconies on to the action apparently at the heart of the rig, although the computer games, of course, actually take place on various monitors. This post-industrial architecture is additionally enhanced by wailing sound effects, naked flame torches, white steam, and greenish, dim lighting. An almost tangible dampness makes many of the surfaces appear slick and glossy; and this, in association with the apparent heaviness of the set along with (occasionally) blocked sight-lines and varying sound levels, makes the set appear both unearthly (spooky) but also, in an almost tactile sense, material. As a total effect, it could be argued that the set aptly functions as a kind of post-industrial, gladiatorial combat zone, the virtual environment of many computer games made real.

What the excessive set belies, or perhaps compensates for, is that the 'combat' itself is generally a very limited affair. Most games involve a rather short task—not longer than two minutes—set by the Gamesmaster, or a short battle (or game) between a celebrity and a contestant. In many ways, the tasks function more as demonstrations than competitions. As a result of this, the actual game play, is, for the most part, rather unexciting. Some additional excitement is clearly needed, and so the presenter, Dominik Diamond, goes up a level in the set and joins an expert—a journalist from one of the numerous computer game magazines—and both then commentate on the progress of the players. This commentary varies between basic information as to where the competitors should go and how much time they have remaining, to other, more arcane, observations concerning the kind of tricks and skills needed to make the jumps, twists, and shooting skills that the game demands.

These discussions of game play and Diamond's general performance as host are particularly distinctive. Echoing the language used in computer game magazines and to an extent the linguistic style favoured by many of the games, Diamond's performance is in a mode best categorized as a kind of sophisticated puerility. He employs a hybrid of straightforward 'comic speak' (in particular, children's comics such as *Dandy* and *Beano*), crossed with the toilet humour and saucy style of British 'seaside postcards'—a combination successfully revamped by the adult comic, *Viz*. The low culture tone of these different media sources is then occasionally punctuated with highbrow allusions. Examples of this style can be seen below as Diamond first introduces a *Gamesmaster* theme day (which was to take place as a special event at the Birmingham NEC):

'Now, unless you've had your head buried in a lavatory basin for the last four weeks you should know that the most pant-wettingly brilliant day is nearly upon us.'

Similarly, the same tone is used when in one programme he is obliged to 'banish' an unsuccessful game player:

'While Lisa acclimatizes to her new found life in the Stygian depths we'll take a look at this week's reviews.'

In both instances, Diamond's patter directs itself to a particular audience; the viewer is presumably thought to be 'in the know' and familiar with this kind of linguistic style. While he (or she) apparently appreciates a metaphor such as 'pant-wettingly brilliant', they will also feel comfortable with a relatively arcane reference to Greek mythology.

Brooker's description of the 'Tomb Raider' game also employs this kind of language; it is a style that presumes a consensus as to which things are likely to be 'pants' (bad) and which things are 'rather spiffy' (good, but said with a large amount of sarcasm). This mode is significant as it is indicative of the adolescent tone of the programme and the computer game culture the programme wishes to validate. It suggests that while knowledge and verbal sophistication are not made legitimate in ways that might be recognized by mainstream culture—or dominant forms of education—there is a sense in which certain kinds of knowledge, or the appearance of having specific kinds of knowledge are championed.

The notion of an 'apparent' knowledge, or knowingness, is a key factor; for while it is unlikely that many viewers would actually know all of the references that are strewn through Diamond's eclectic patter, I think they would neither show, nor worry, about their ignorance. As part of a performance this kind of language is also important as it became established as a distinctive or even definitive characteristic of many youth television performers and presenters. It also has links with the kind of 'extreme inter-textuality' that John Caldwell identifies in relation to *Pee-Wee's Playhouse*.[17] However, in relation to *Gamesmaster*, it is yet another aspect which links the programme firmly to the computer game itself. It reproduces part of what Stallabrass describes as an essential element of the computer game experience:

As with the exploitation of 'heritage' themes, many of the game elements are familiar since childhood and are recognized at once. They are collected, combined and packaged as entertainment,

17 John T. Caldwell, *Televisuality: Style, Crisis and Authority in American Television* (New Brunswick, NJ: Rutgers University Press, 1995), 218–19.

inevitably with a strong flavour of pastiche. The experience is evocative rather than informative since the past is represented by 'archetypal' codes—the twenties by jazz music, prehistory by some Raquel Welch figure in a fur bikini. It is not so much the stuff of history as of television series and pulp novels. This is essential because, as we have seen, the operation of these games is largely parasitic upon other media and half-remembered scenes are an important foundation for the players' emotional engagement.[18]

Diamond's script and performance, as well as the structure of the show itself, are, like the games Stallabrass is describing here, evocative rather than informative. This means that the kind of knowledge demanded and celebrated by the show is built up through fragments, through in-jokes and common assumptions; engagement and learning are based on half-remembered forms, fictions, and facts originating in other media and may include certain allusions and references that are only understood later, if at all. I want to suggest that this kind of learning and engagement may encourage a relationship to the text that is 'magpie-like', and perhaps points to the development of a *bricolage* mentality. In this instance different individuals, presented with an abundance of information, noise, and spectacle, learn to tune into only those specific elements that are useful or pleasurable and may simply gawk at or ignore aspects that remain incomprehensible.

This viewing style is suggested by Sherry Turkle's observations, in her recent book *Life on the Screen: Identity in the Age of the Internet.* In the chapter, 'The Triumph of Tinkering', she describes a similar intellectual and emotional style as a methodology that she has observed people adopting in response to the problem of computer programming. Describing a specific approach to programming as 'tinkering', she presents it as a 'soft' style, in contrast to the 'hard' approach previously favoured within the 'analytic methodology of Western science'.[19] At one point, she recalls Claude Levi-Strauss's work on non-Western scientific practices; observing the non-Western scientist (the 'medicine man') working through, and with, the 'objects at hand' in order to make a diagnosis, Levi-Strauss interprets his behaviour as a form of *bricolage.* Turkle notes:

> By analogy, problem-solvers who do not proceed from top-down design but by arranging and re-arranging a set of well-known materials can be said to be practising bricolage. They tend to try one thing, step back, reconsider, and try another. For planners

18 Stallabrass, 'Just Gaming', 93.

19 Sherry Turkle, *Life on the Screen: Identity in the Age of the Internet* (London: Weidenfeld & Nicolson, 1996), 51.

[those who have mastered the 'hard' and legitimate approach], mistakes are steps in the wrong direction; bricoleurs navigate through midcourse corrections. Bricoleurs approach problem-solving by entering into a relationship with their work materials that has more the flavor of a conversation than a monologue.[20]

Turkle then goes on to relate this specifically to the activity of the computer game player who engages with a simulated environment that has become increasingly opaque.

In recent years, the designers of video games have been pushing the games further into realistic simulation through graphics, animation, sound, and interactivity. And in recent years, games, like other aspects of computing, have become more opaque. Like the Macintosh desktop, video games for most players carry ideas about a world one does not so much analyze as inhabit . . .
As in other opaque simulations, the surface of the game takes precedence over what lies beneath. As one eighteen-year old player put it, 'It doesn't feel so much like solving a puzzle as living in a puzzle'.[21]

The key aspect here, for my purposes, is her notion that the player 'inhabits' the game; the player's ambition is therefore less tied up in the resolution of the game and more concerned with an adaptation to the game environment. In relation to this, I believe that the viewers who are most appropriate, as well as those who are most likely to enjoy *Gamesmaster*, do so by submitting to the overarching environment of the programme. An environment, which is constructed through the *mise en scène*, Diamond's performance, and the individual's own knowledge of the games and related programmes. The absence of analysis on the part of such viewers (-as-players) suggests that even if all the aspects of the programme are not strictly pleasing or com-prehensible to the viewer, this is not distressing, as control, mastery, or a need for total understanding is no longer the primary ambition. Information that is either incomprehensible or redundant will simply be glossed over, leaving the viewer untroubled, but also none the wiser. If we were therefore to try to fit *Gamesmaster* into the previous model of the television game show, it might be possible to suggest that the programme, like other game shows, engenders a context where a specific kind of knowledge is validated. However, *Gamesmaster* is dif-ferent because the knowledge it celebrates is functional and specific to a particular subculture. Although the knowledge it draws on is in some senses empirical and social, it is also limited, partial, and fuzzy. The emphasis in the programme is not on 'right' or 'wrong' answers,

20 Ibid., 51.
21 Ibid., 68.

or in the perfection of skills that may be more generally applicable, but a gradual and repetitive revelation of the moves and cheats needed so that games may be completed in a faster time. Although there are hints that there is some kind of resolution to be had in the programme, it is a conclusion that must not and cannot be sustained. Other aspects of *Gamesmaster*, for example, urge the viewer-as-player to make another purchase so that they are obliged to begin yet another—and often very similar—game.

Gamesmaster is also different from many traditional game shows as there is clear evidence that morals and ethics have also become ambivalent. This is because it has become more difficult (or unimportant) for the player/viewer to separate the 'true' from the 'false', or fact from fiction. Turkle, for example, argues:

> Games such as SimLife teach players to think in an active way about complex phenomena (some of them 'real life', some of them not) as dynamic, evolving systems. But they also encourage people to get used to manipulating a system whose core assumptions they do not see and which may or may not be 'true'.[22]

In the context of *Gamesmaster* the kind of knowledge that is celebrated is not that which serves to make you wiser—that which provides a greater understanding of the world, or even, simply, improves your 'general' knowledge. Rather it is a knowledge which makes you seem smarter, in that it allows you to feel and/or pretend that you are an insider in relation to the computer game culture. Questions concerning legitimate and illegitimate forms of knowledge, or the validation of truth claims, are, as Turkle suggests in relation to her own study, irrelevant.

This *bricoleur* approach in relation to television viewing is very much akin to television viewing as 'garage-sale foraging' as identified by John T. Caldwell in his book *Televisuality: Style, Crisis and Authority in American Television*. He describes this approach as a form of viewing that he believes is necessitated or engendered by the various programmes that he categorizes as 'trash TV'. He uses the metaphor of the 'thrift store' or the 'garage-sale' to suggest how an individual may approach the abundance of textual references, knowing asides, high and low culture allusions, or even the sheer plethora of 'things' that might confront them as a 'trash TV' viewer:

> As any weekend warrior will tell you, garage-sale foraging demands as much cultural distinction and buyer discrimination as any form of television auteurism.[23]

22 Ibid., 70.
23 Caldwell, *Televisuality*, 193–4.

The skills of the garage-sale fanatic include the ability to 'pick and mix', and an ability to rapidly 'sort through' an apparent jumble of information and/or material. Successful foraging will involve the possibility of mistakes; in any event, it will always require individuals to be able to filter through, and make sense of, a 'mess' of material. All of these skills are necessary if these 'second-hand' consumers are to produce successful combinations (of clothes, objects, etc.) and make purchasing decisions that are useful, or at least make sense to them in a way that is pleasurable. *Gamesmaster* demands a similarly informed process of negotiation, as it, too, presents the viewer with an abundance of material, information, noise, and spectacle. Although each specific environment (the computer game, the thrift store, and each individual's viewing situation) will produce different permutations of such tactics, in *Gamesmaster* the competition centres on the computer game. Because the games used in the programme are available to buy, the viewer too can also become the competitor or player. The play in *Gamesmaster* therefore requires or demonstrates that the competitor on screen and the viewer (who is potentially a player) master certain qualities and skills. Firstly, at the start of each new game, players will need to remain unfazed by the abundance of information and by the detailed spectacle of the game so that they can concentrate on play and tactics. Secondly, as the game progresses, players will need to be persistent as they need to keep trying, and to keep experimenting, even if they keep failing at specific points in the game, and even when they have no distinct idea how they are to proceed. This means that the narrative they produce will often be circular and repetitive rather than logical and linear. Thirdly, most games used and promoted by the show require that players remember trivial pieces of information (such as the location of magic keys and the remembering of passwords), and practise specific and elaborate skills (such as the somersaults or special jumps and turns required to kill specific attackers.) All of these factors are part of a gradual acclimatization to the environment of the game. Rather than an holistic approach, learning in this instance is represented as idiosyncratic, piecemeal, problem based, and it is also fuzzy (meaning that it is not always thought through), and it may appear instinctive rather than logical. It is also partial, in the sense that it is both fragmentary and specific to each player who appears on the show, who, nevertheless, becomes anonymous as he or she submits to the overall architecture of each computer game played.

In some senses, this kind of attitude is post-modern. Seen from a wider context it may be a response to a culture or a world where it is no longer possible to 'know everything' (or, even, to 'know of' every-thing) with any degree of confidence. The partiality of the knowledge needed and celebrated by *Gamesmaster* reveals that the kind of education that is being validated by the show is not universal or universalizing, or, indeed, even concrete and distinct. Rather, it demonstrates that valuable knowledge is functional knowledge, and in this instance is revealed to be knowledge that is purposeful and specific, even devious or self-serving. For in *Gamesmaster* the real purpose is to direct the player/viewer to make purchasing decisions, or to get to where he (or she) wishes to go, in a game they may already own.

Despite the linguistic exuberance, and the spectacular appeal of *Gamesmaster*, there is a sense in which even the interested viewer (that is, one who has some investment in the computer game) may find many parts of the programme redundant. Many of the reviews concern games that do not run on every system and tips or cheats relating to individual games will not just be irrelevant, but are possibly incomprehensible to viewers who are not familiar with the game in question. For the *bricoleur* viewer, however, these bits of information will not necessarily be upsetting or irritating as they are integrated into the environment of the show. Understood primarily from an aesthetic standpoint and therefore as spectacle each item may be apt and exciting as long as they are consistent with the overall *mise en scène* of the programme. As Caldwell suggests, in relation to 'trash' television programmes:

> They [the programmes] all seek to overwhelm the viewer not with narrative or history, but with physical stuff and frenetic action. From a systems theory point of view, this kind of communication is dominated by informational noise. There simply is no background. Everything is channelled up front. Seen from the perspective of the garage-sale aesthetic mastered by many discriminating viewers, however, this kind of spatial overload is one of the chief pleasures that comes from the televisual tube.[24]

There are several ways that *Gamesmaster* can be seen to produce its own version of 'spatial overload'. Initially the contrast between the virtual location and the detailed material depths of the set provide one distinctive and spatial peculiarity to the programme. Different items within *Gamesmaster* also make up for a 'lack of narrative' in themselves with a form of spectacle that relies heavily on a constant play between depth and flatness, and between the different 'places' seemingly created and opened up to the viewer. The review section of the programme is located within a virtual picture frame (or computer console), through which the reviewer's face (in extreme close-up) can be seen. The increased depth or interest that this gives the screen compensates, perhaps, for any loss of interest. This may stem either from the fact that many of the reviews are essentially the same—because in

---

24 Ibid., 193.

effect many of the games are too—or from the fact that the game is not one that can be played on the viewer's own system. There are also instances where it is clear that the video of the reviewer has been 'fast-forwarded' (this is seen on screen) and this demonstrates the programme's play with the image, and its explicit wish to skip through the 'boring bits', thereby mimicking the audience's own viewing activities. Another place in which depth and an attention to spectacle is highlighted is in the tips or 'cheats' section, where the questioner dons a 'virtuality' mask supposedly to enter the Gamesmaster's virtual realm, so that the viewer is then able to see them materialize on to a digitized background.

The visual excess of each element or sequence within the show is also enhanced by a constant movement between these various different 'places'. Throughout the programme frequent camera pans add movement and pace to the show, especially as this often involves the camera apparently following participants as they move between different levels of the set. There are also another series of movements dictated by the virtual and screen-based game play; these involve a shift of focus into, and on to, different screens—the Gamesmaster's realm, the different computer monitors, and the big video screens that also feature in the set. Following Caldwell's arguments, it seems likely that this spatial abundance provides an excitement that is designed to compensate for the relative paucity of actual competition.

The lack of actual competition within the programme also suggests that the kind of viewing perspective encouraged by *Gamesmaster* is not aspirational in the traditional sense that is usually associated with the game show. It does not involve the generation of a suspenseful narrative; for questions such as 'Who will win?' or 'Will they solve the puzzle or get the right answers?' are largely irrelevant. There is also no discernible (or external) profit to be made by the competitors if they are successful. Rather than enabling the viewer to 'escape', knowledge of computer games will encourage them to become entrenched again in yet another game. Diamond's role, therefore, is not that of a traditional game show host; and he is not interested in asking contestants to display skills that may then be translated into capital in the form of consumer goods. Instead, Diamond provides a central focus for an environment where, although a prize—the golden joystick—can indeed be won, the real excitement for the viewer does not stem from empathizing with the contestants—there are few things more boring, after all, than watching someone else play a computer game. Instead the appeal of the show lies in the way in which it both reveals, and lets the viewer in on, an inclusive (and therefore exclusive) subculture.

The *Gamesmaster* world is bizarre and, to the uninitiated viewer as well as the committed computer game player, the overall affect of the programme is exotic, even fantastic. At the same time it is half-familiar (half-remembered and parasitic on other media) and this means that, more often than not, the terrors and the pleasures it calls up are also innocuous. For while the programme and the games themselves display safely packaged monsters, oddities, and adventures these are all contained, explored, and gently satirized.

A similarly exotic package-deal is reproduced by the *Crystal Maze*. This time, however, the journeys made by the contestants must employ skills that are real rather than vicarious, and (physically) material rather than virtual. The *Crystal Maze* is a relatively straightforward hybrid of computer game aesthetics combined with a series of physical and mental tasks. Six young adult contestants form a team who must follow their host through four interconnected zones, each of which contains different games or tasks which must be successfully completed in order to win 'crystals'. Each crystal grants the players five seconds in the large crystal dome at the end of each show. Once in the dome, the team attempts to collect gold tokens (which are whirling around them) in order to win a weekend break or short activity holiday. The maze, like the *Gamesmaster*'s oil rig resort, is virtual; although each section is an elaborate piece of set, the show provides a simulated blueprint to suggest how the various zones are fitted together. This blueprint is seen when the transition between the zones is managed by a cut to a computer graphic representing the imaginary map of the maze; within this, a flashing red light illustrates where the next destination is to be. This diagrammatic illustration, (supplemented by electronic, pulsing, incidental music) along with a brief sequence showing contestants crossing a bridge or passing through a tunnel, stitches the virtual architecture of the maze and the diverse material sections together. During the history of the programme, these zones have differed; however, in the programme that I will be citing as an example (from the 1992 series), the zones are Aztec, futuristic, medieval, and industrial. Each zone is elaborately dressed to be appropriate to each period and the games within each section are tailored to fit with the 'look' of each zone. For example, a game involving a heraldic jigsaw puzzle featured in the medieval zone, while a simple wooden raft featured in a physical game from the Aztec section. Yet each look was not entirely distinct, consistent, or historically accurate; a piano for instance featured in the medieval section, while the futuristic and industrial zones (both characterized by lots of metal and clunky architecture) were very similar to one another.

It should be clear from this brief description the extent to which the series echoes many of the identifying characteristics of the computer game; different exotic zones (that are themselves pastiche-like simulations) are subdivided into smaller territories where a variety of tasks have to be completed. The similarity between the two forms is increased by the fact that if a competitor runs out of time, or is simply unable to complete the task, they will be 'locked in' (literally stuck) at that section of the maze. This of course means that they are then unable to progress to other zones or to other tasks with the rest of their team-mates. Appropriately, and again like many computer games, contestants may only be released if one of the crystals is sacrificed. This again closely mimics many computer games where a player is unable to progress or get past a particular point in the game unless they complete a specific task either within, or at, a specific time.

The *Crystal Maze*'s dependence for cohesion upon a central figure —an omniscient 'master'—is similarly reminiscent of computer games. Richard O'Brien, the creator of the cult film and stage musical *The Rocky Horror Show* (1975), hosts the show as a bald, camp, and sarcastic dandy. In contrast with the excitability, engagement, and good humour of the traditional game show host, O'Brien appears to be bored, cynical, and petulant. In addition to this, he portrays a kind of 'other worldly' innocence and is, at times, irritatingly whimsical.[25] While O'Brien's role is primarily to lead competitors around the maze and to set tasks (and, at points, to give hints and to keep the time) he does much more than this. His teasing of the competitors, direct asides to camera, and observations about the maze itself all serve to disrupt what might have otherwise been a simple revamp of a more traditional game show such as *The Krypton Factor* or, worse, a straightforward televisation of executive 'training weekends'. O'Brien's performance allows him to show open disrespect for the competitors, who were either mostly students or employed in a variety of middle-class occupations, including chemists, computer programmers, and even aeroplane pilots. At times, for example, he might gently mock them for playing badly—'That's not very good is it?'—or even openly yawn when play was slow.

In part this attitude stems from the fact that the competitors (unlike O'Brien) remain largely anonymous, and are less likely to be subject to identification or empathy by the television viewer. They are easy, or acceptable, targets, for O'Brien's ridicule. For while contestants are introduced briefly at the beginning of the programme (in a simulation of a computer file/police record, O'Brien reports their name, age, and occupation) there is little, or no, informal 'chit-chat' either between team-mates, or between individual contestants and O'Brien. Neither the rapport established by a host such as Michael Barrymore, nor the scripted stand-up comedian performances of other game show hosts such as Bob Monkhouse, takes place. The competitors' lack of individuality is also exacerbated by the way

---

25 In later series, the tradition continued when O'Brien was replaced by the equally eccentric Edward Tudor from the defunct punk rock group Ten Pole Tudor.

they are dressed: all the contestants wear similar (although differently coloured) tracksuits, so that they present a uniform appearance, in stark contrast to O'Brien's eccentric dress. Rather than adopting the 'school master' or anonymous attire of the traditional game show host—the suit and tie—O'Brien favours frock coats with leopard skin lapels, patterned cowboy boots, and tight trousers that accentuate his skinny physique. This bizarre outfit seems appropriate within the spectacular environment of the set, and, conversely, also serves to increase the anonymity of the contestants. In fact, the contestants could even be seen to represent the on-screen representative of the computer game player. The function of the player as icon has been usefully described by Gillian Skirrow in her article, 'Hellivision: An Analysis of Video Games'. The lack of individuality on the part of such icons or figures, she argues, suggests that:

> the emphasis or at least all the interest, is in that predicate, the paranoiac environment. The performer himself has no character traits that are not causal—because he is adventurous, he has an adventure—and, needless to say, there is no development of character as the game progresses. It is the game that controls, as the 'dungeon master' or 'Destinateur', with the performer as only a function of its flow.[26]

In relation to the *Crystal Maze* this suggests that the viewer is not obliged to empathize with, or concentrate on, the fate of the contestants, but instead invests imaginatively in the vivid, 'paranoiac' environment constructed through the programme's *mise en scène* and articulated in the performance of O'Brien as host. Although the show is clearly akin to other game shows such as *Gladiators* and *The Generation Game*, the *Crystal Maze* is not interested in allowing the contestants to be understood outside the context of the game— they do not have families or idiosyncratic personality traits. This allows the programme to be meaner to the competitors and prevents any serious displeasure in the relatively high failure rate of most of the teams. While I am tempted to argue that there may an anti-'yuppie' agenda here, this is unlikely to be a deliberate policy of the programme itself. However, a hint of subversion may be detected in some of the programmes. In one show a pilot is featured as the team captain. At 36, he is older than his team-mates, and, as a result of this, he seems initially (and perhaps unwisely) to be establishing a greater presence for himself than is usual for a contestant in the show. He even dares to respond with a mildly daring 'What ever you say, baby' to one of O'Brien's more camp outbursts. This bid for individuality or

---

26 Gillian Skirrow, 'Hellivision: An Analysis of Video Games', reprinted in M. Alvarado and J. O. Thompson (eds.), *The Media Reader* (London: British Film Institute, 1990), 330.

spontaneity does not go unpunished. O'Brien's put-down—'Come Fly with me . . . indeed?'—is delivered shortly thereafter, when it becomes clear that the hapless pilot is trapped, locked in one of the puzzle rooms. As the pilot's time limit expires, O'Brien becomes openly gleeful. Not all of the rooms are designed to confine a failing contestant, and it is O'Brien who assigns the task to each one. In short, foul play is suspected. This potential for malevolence provides another reason as to why the show is popular with a youth audience and, even more predominantly, children; the show clearly allows for the illicit enjoyment of seeing these people fail, a pleasure increased by the fact that a substantial proportion of the competitors occupy positions of authority in the real world—many of them are teachers.

O'Brien's inconsistent approach to both the game and the con-testants is distinguished by his use of direct address; in particular, in his insincere-sincere asides to the camera. On the one hand his comments ask the audience to accept the fantasy of the show as he claims to have made all the games himself—'with these little hands'—and to live in the maze with various 'Aunties'. On the other hand, he acknowledges the impossibility of believing him when he comments with faux innocence that 'You can take it from me, that what I say is absolutely gospel.' Certainly his performance is arch enough for even the most uninterested viewer to recognize that this is not to be taken seriously. At other points he may play a piano and sing directly to camera while a game is being completed—mostly unseen. It is worth quoting one ditty in full here, as it provides a succinct illustration of O'Brien's self-reflexivity and ironic detachment. Having cleared the piano keyboard of a dead mouse, he sings:

> 'Who has a show full of social irrelevance?
> Who do you know with so-so intelligence?
> Who makes his dough with a flow of no eloquence?
> Yes, I guess, I'm talking about me.'

Yet, while O'Brien appears unable to contain his boredom with the show and seemingly demonstrates that he believes the programme to be worthless, his inconsistent performance contains various con-tradictions. While he certainly plays the fool, his position as master of the maze also allows him to know more than the competitors—meaning that he is knowledgeable, as well as knowing. So, on the one hand, his performance suggests that he wants the viewing audience to understand that the show presents an illusion, on the other hand, he continually refers to, and develops the fantasy of, the maze as a real place. As a host, therefore, O'Brien has to be trusted, as he knows how things work, and how to get to different zones, but at the same time, he is deceitful and therefore untrustworthy—as he tells lies and makes up stories. This creates a sense of ambivalence for the viewer as the demands of the programme seemingly encourage levels of investment and empathy that are at odds with one another. O'Brien's attitude suggests that the viewer would be foolish to take the game seriously. Yet in other ways the show is clearly designed to encourage viewers to take more than a passing interest, or to make more than a casual investment in the concept and overall *mise en scène* of the programme. The level of detail in the various sections of the maze, including the attention to the right sound effects, lighting and texture, as well as a camera style which encourages a sense in which the set is both deep and fully realized—as the camera swoops down into each level, and then follows the contestants around each section in a jerky, hand-held manner—work to pull the viewer in emotionally and cognitively. This attention to detail means that the viewer may (despite O'Brien's cynicism) feel genuine pleasure in relation to the spectacle presented by the programme. And this is a pleasure that will not be diminished by the detachment (or even scorn) that they may feel in relation to the contestants.

The *Crystal Maze* and *Gamesmaster* both present and privilege their embracing *mise en scènes*. The distinctive aesthetic of both programmes produces a pastiche architecture that supports an eclectic hybrid of different media forms masquerading as a specific culture or game. Each show alludes to other television game shows, films, comics, and, predominantly, computer games, and these are all reproduced and situated within the different spaces that are located within the context of the fake place of each programme. Television game shows, of course, were never original but what makes these two programmes distinctive is the sheer extent to which they have been fully realized as alternative dimensions for a particular kind of investment and fantasy. Both programmes seem to be concerned to champion a constant (and repetitive) negotiation, or assimilation with, an environment that seemingly threatens to overwhelm the contestant and, perhaps, the viewer. In these shows, the traditional game show narrative has been replaced by repetitive fragments that are marked by an excessive manipulation of space and a high degree of detailed visual spectacle.

Another distinctive characteristic is that, while there is no sense in which these programmes are truly subversive, as game shows they both differ from more traditional versions of the genre because they are morally, and perhaps ideologically, ambivalent. Although both shows are clearly caught up with, and participate in, the commodification of fantasy, knowledge, and skill, there is also a sense in which they are knowing and cynical about this process. These programmes do not, therefore, offer themselves as utopian or carnivalesque visions of a truly egalitarian, opportunistic, capitalist society. What they do, however, is suggest ways of coping with a commodified culture. This is suggested particularly by the way in which both the shows call on and elaborate aspects of the computer game culture and the computer game itself and, specifically perhaps, the mixed emotions and multi-valent uses that this technology inspires. The kind of process and pleasure I am alluding to is represented in Ruth Furlong's descriptive study of a small group of young boys and their relation to computer games (and other media):

> Despite the addictiveness of computer games, the boys were unable to articulate the pleasure they gained from playing them. They reported that they quickly became bored with a particular scenario and the activity became relegated from an obsession to an activity mostly indulged in 'when friends came round'. In this sense they seemed cynically aware that the aim of the games' promoters was that after consuming one, they would desire another. Their talk in relation to such games was much more related to the principles of capitalism and forms of resistance (sharing, copying, bartering and varying machine use between households) than to content and fantasy locations.[27]

While the programmes do not generate the obsession generated by the games—they are not interactive in the same way—what they can do is validate and celebrate the knowledge, attitude, and skills that have become associated with the computer game. Both programmes thereby generate a sensibility akin to the informed irony that I have repeatedly suggested may be a characteristic of Generation X. This sensibility calls upon, and generates, a peculiar accumulation of information, understanding, and emotion that has accrued through a familiarity and intimacy with various media, and with television in particular. The programmes present an elaborate and detailed spectacle that is also, in some senses, incomplete. In order to fill in the gaps, and engage with the text, the viewer must bring into play their own palimpsest of emotion and cognition. This process thereby encourages viewers to identify (or 'forage') a particular, individualized strategy in relation to what they want either from the programme in question or, perhaps, from the wider aspects of the popular culture the programmes allude to. In effect, what both the *Crystal Maze* and *Gamesmaster* seem to provide is a representation of an environment where it is possible, and even admirable, to 'buy in' while, seemingly, 'opting out' of visions, activities, and pleasures that are known to be commercial and (as Furlong's observations suggest) ultimately unsatisfactory. What the programmes represent is a way of combining these apparently contradictory impulses through an understanding (and potentially an adoption) of a performance style, or habitual mode which incorporates both cynicism and (a magical and technological) enchantment.

27 Ruth Furlong, 'There's No Place Like Home', in M. Lister (ed.), *The Photographic Image in Digital Culture* (London and New York: Routledge, 1995), 180.

5

The 'Television Presenter' The Post-modern Performer

I T is notoriously difficult to describe accurately the experience of watching television—not just how you watch, but how you feel, and why you feel, when you watch. This is important for any assessment of television texts, but it is central in the assessment and analysis of a performance that is so strongly encoded by extra-textual elements. The specificity of the experience of 'watching television' is missed not only because the domestic situation is very difficult to report or fully understand, and not just because the family dynamics and disinterested 'gaze' of the so-called typical television viewer can be misrepresented. This is true of all media that are characterized by their sociability; what is also lacking, and what concerns me here, is a way to encapsulate in any useful form the kind of experience that Generation X will have accrued by years of watching. It is, I want to suggest, the cumulating of viewing experiences that will inform their television viewing in significant ways, ways that are specific to television as an aesthetic and technological form. It is the kind of experience which in some large part determines the pleasure and the meaning of television watching, and it is not easily understood or represented because so much viewing is not rational or systematic, but is, instead, a knowledge built out of familiarity and happenstance. It is a process of accumulation: it is a developing 'inner voice' or a 'mental echo', both emotional and cognitive, that is generated by expectation and repetition. Watching and interpreting television texts and television performances for me, and many of the young television viewers I have been describing in this study, is articulated by an ongoing passive/active participation, and by the encroachment of years of television viewing.

One possible way of describing what I mean by this kind of knowledge would be to suggest that it is like hearing the beginning of a particular piece of music when, because of your familiarity with the order of tracks on a favourite album, you anticipate the first few notes of the next song after the last, and are then surprised when the tape playing in the shop, or the DJ's play list, does not go on to reproduce the sounds that are stubbornly playing in your head. In relation to television, the almost unconscious construction of anticipation and expectation, or the experiential knowledge possessed by each viewer, will ultimately be defined by the individual's habits, prejudices, and simply how much television they have watched. However, it is also associated with factors that the individual may share with others, specifically, the *when, where,* and *how* of the viewing context. *When* you watched refers, of course, to decades, historical periods, fashions, to solar eclipses, moon landings, and political elections, but also, mundanely, to what time of day, and with whom you watched. Equally important is *where* you watched (both domestically and geographically) and *how* you watched, which is likely to have differed considerably over time. The expectations and assumptions generated by the kind of television experienced by the young viewer will necessarily inform their understanding and appreciation of performance, of the acting and appearing that occurs on the small screen; it frames both feeling and taste.

In this attempt to describe a particular kind of performance on the small screen I will be obliged to spend the majority of my time explaining things that are *not* the performance (that is *how* and *what* actually happens) and will, inevitably, be obliged to reveal my own television viewing experiences. The difficulty that arises from this is that I cannot guarantee that I can read every instance fully, similarly I cannot be certain that the youth audience were able to pick up on some of the references I see as key. Such difficulties are often at their most acute when we are looking at performances as parody or homage: in relation to some viewers, for example, it may be that they have only witnessed Madonna in the video for 'Material Girl' playing Marilyn Monroe, and have never seen Monroe playing Lorelei in *Gentlemen Prefer Blondes* (1953). Or, equally, they may not realize that Keanu Reeves in the Paula Abdul video 'Push, Push' is playing James Dean, as Dean played Jim Stark in *Rebel Without a Cause* (1955). The problem is not just one of research or presentation; obviously, while it is feasible to research and reproduce specific moments it is harder to engender, or demonstrate their *significance,* whether emotional or social. The kind of experience I am describing is not just the accumulation of evidence (the seeing of films and television programmes); it is also, in part, a social and emotional experience, weathered and fitted into the individual psyche. Yet it is precisely these generational references that are central to the performances of the yoof presenters I have discussed and will explore further in this chapter. References to certain television programmes, films, the stars, and the celebrities, as well as the kind of biographical, historical information that is taken for granted, serve to distinguish the way in which this audience understands the nature and perform-ance style of the different presenters that directly appeal to them. I have discussed several presenters in other parts of this book; here, however, I will focus on Chris Evans, who is perhaps the most suc-cessful proponent of the yoof style.

Since Evans's role is as host or presenter his reference points—and the audience's—must be the pre-existing mainstream forms of presentation on television, characterized by an emphasis on direct address. There are two dominant forms here: firstly journalistic, as employed by newscasters, reporters, and documentary presenters. Within this there are also two distinct styles. The first of these is rep-resented by the newscaster or reader: this style is reproduced by the authoritative, modulated, and static performances of news-readers such as Michael Buerk or Jon Snow, who rely heavily upon the voice (usually deep, and retaining the RP accent of the traditional BBC announcer) and who are (mostly) immobile, with, for example, the news-reader positioned behind a desk. Their hands are rarely seen and the presence and movement of news-readers' hands on screen either indicates a conclusion to the performance (the shuffling of papers at the end of the newscast) or a mistake (a televised report unavailable or miscued), forcing the reader to reach for an alternat-ive story or script. When readers are obliged to question reporters and politicians both within and without the studio, both voice and posture may occasionally move to the mildly interrogative; what is expressed here is an urgency and liveness suggested through an increase in pace and voice level, and by the reader physically turning, or leaning forward to the interviewee. However, the dominant mode is distinguished by the news-reader 'holding' the look of the camera, involving an almost unblinking eye contact in his or her attempt to address the viewer directly at home. This is, of course, an illusion sustained by the autocue, enabling the reader to look up and read from the script at the same time.[1]

In contrast to this, we can identify the anchor of a magazine cur-rent affairs programme, or the presenter of a documentary series. In Britain this would include performers such as Jeremy Paxman, Peter Snow, or Kirsty Wark on *Newsnight*, Robin Day and now David Dimbleby on *Question Time*, or David Attenborough presenting a natural history series such as *Life On Earth*. Though authoritative (and still predominantly masculine, and RP in accent) these per-formers are more mobile and excitable. Using a greater range of voice

1 The changes that have recently involved a greater amount of mobility for news-readers—particularly on Channel 4—can be directly linked to the success of the youthful style of news presentation established by Kirsty Young on Channel 5.

—from a whisper in David Attenborough's case, to the high pitched hysteria of an excited Peter Snow—these leaders or seekers are allowed much more space and time to perform. Their hands are much more visible, and both Wark and Paxman, for example, use their fingers to point and ask leading questions. Similarly, Attenborough leaps and scrabbles in his 'natural environment', playing nervously, for example, with a family of gorillas or crouching down and into the camera lens, so that he is absurdly close both to the watching audience and to the object of his attention, in one instance, a tiny Arctic flower. The 'seeker' therefore reaches and points to the animate and inanimate— politicians and flowers. These performers have to force information from their surroundings, creating particular pressures, which show up in their performance. Peter Snow's hysteria, as he manipulates graphics displaying voting predictions, or when he plays with tanks in a mock-up of Desert Storm, is laughable because we can see clearly that most of the information that he is revealing is redundant, irrelevant, and conjectural. Or, in the case of a long election night special, not *there* (where he is pointing) yet. In these contexts, the seeker's excitability is a bid to keep our attention, but it is also a poor mask for their desperation. These performers may also develop verbal tics just as they develop familiar physical mannerisms—Jeremy Paxman's 'Come off it' or 'With respect, Minister', as responses indicating his increasing irritation, have become infamous. Over months and even years of familiarity with these tics and foibles the audience may accept them as characters, allowing Jeremy Paxman, for example, more latitude for aggression or cynicism, as part of his expected and accepted performance, than we would admire, or allow, from another journalist performer.

The other dominant form of direct address, and closely related to the journalistic style, are the performances of presenters such as Anne Diamond and Nick Owen (from the BBC's *Good Morning . . . with Anne and Nick*, and Richard and Judy of *This Morning*. Weaned on Breakfast television and regional presenting, these performers are more relaxed than their journalistic contemporaries, yet their performance is still in some sense a 'cover up'. Their performances embody contradictions: at once knowing and friendly, open and polished, they include and charm their audience. They welcome the viewer in, pretty much with open arms, particularly in the context of daytime magazine or breakfast shows where they are obliged to reveal more than their news associates, so that sometimes all of the body is on display and available to the viewer. Very often this can mean that the female presenter's body—like Lorraine Kelly's, Oprah Winfrey's, or Rikki Lake's—feature as an important locus for some aspects of their discussion, and act as the basis of their authenticity and connection to their viewing audience.

While presenters may address the viewer at home, they also look at each other (play off one another, and visibly appreciate each other's performances) so that at moments they may enter into a music hall or vaudeville style, a comedic performance taken to its extreme in the stand-up performance of Chris Evans (in *The Big Breakfast*) generously supported by the giggling or 'corpsing' straightman, as played by Gaby Roslin. Whether manic or relaxed, the presenter as operator of the magazine show produces a skilful performance that is defined by control (hence, in part the 'cover up', which covers gaps, drops in pace, or weak performances from guests) so that even seemingly radical performers such as Evans admire mainstream, and seemingly conservative, 'professionals' such as Noel Edmunds or Michael Barrymore. As controllers, presenters are also acting as hosts and are therefore aligned to chat show and game show performers; Michael Barrymore and Noel Edmunds, for example, have both performed in, or presented, comedic magazine programmes as well as straightforward game shows.

Since the presenter's performance style has obvious comedic and music hall elements, it is not surprising that numerous 'straight' comedians, have themselves had success as presenters—comedians such as Bob Monkhouse, Roy Walker, and the late Les Dawson effectively presented the lighter versions of game shows. The more authoritative pose or performance of the journalist style can also be seen in game shows that supposedly require a little more education—Jeremy Paxman's hosting of *University Challenge* is unsurprising, just as Magnus Magnusson's (the host of *Mastermind*) occasional documentary presentation does not go against the grain of his performance style.

The other factor behind such cross casting is that familiar faces and their reappearance in a variety of different contexts is very much in accord with television's wish to create an atmosphere of 'sociability'. Television, particularly in its use of direct address, wants the audience to feel that it offers worlds and faces that are familiar, knowable, and therefore somehow accessible to the viewer. Increasingly this is not simply about the relationship between presenters and audience but between presenters themselves and/or their celebrity guests. The real or constructed flirtations between Johnny Vaughan and Denise Van Outen (on *The Big Breakfast*), Gail Porter and Tim Vincent on *Fully Booked*, and Dec and Cat on *SMTV: Live*, foster a sense that the audience is being given access to private liaisons. In its earliest days *The Big Breakfast* worked similarly to titillate its audience in the segment where Paula Yates (known as the wife of Bob Geldof and as a presenter of an earlier music show *The Tube*) would interview selected celebrity guests 'on the bed'. Rather conveniently for the dynamic that this item set up, Yates eventually left Geldof for one of these celebrity guests—Michael Hutchence of the pop group INXS.

Yet the chat show host or television presenter also appears for and with *ordinary* people. How do they (we?) appear, and what can be said about their performance (if it can be called that?)? *How* they appear may be determined by *where* they appear. And ordinary people appear in diverse contexts: performing as 'expert' or eye witness, as victim or perpetrator in the news or documentary, as game show contestants, or simply as accident prone in home-made videos. Ordinary people perform in numerous contexts, and are beginning to appear more and more frequently, and in a wider range of programmes. One of the most interesting recent developments has been the *Video Nation* shorts, where, sandwiched between a dramatic serial and *Newsnight*, the same ordinary person may appear and reappear (albeit briefly) as music enthusiast, lottery loser, and/or political commentator.

Ordinary people are likely to be both constrained and liberated in their performances. In certain contexts they will be more constrained than professional performers as they are more likely to be intimidated by the technology, and the mechanics of being 'on' television. From the audience's perspective, we may hold our breath, sharing their anxiety: we are alternatively with them and against them, anticipating or possibly willing disaster. Our worries concerning the ordinary person will be related to the conventions of the programme context. In the news interview or informal discussion programme we may fear that the ordinary person will freeze, look into the wrong camera lens, or refuse to understand or participate in the agenda of questions. In the game show we may be dismayed or inappropriately amused when we see the ordinary person fluster the host, or disrupt the carefully organized hierarchies of the space taped on to the studio floor. For even in a people-centred game show such as *Blind Date* participants are confined to specific places and pathways, which are strictly patrolled by camera-angles, floor managers, and ultimately Cilla Black, the host. *Blind Date* is a particularly useful example, as it demonstrates another concern for the ordinary person: the pressure to win sympathy and the work required to get the 'laugh'; an ability largely determined in this case by Cilla herself, who may support or undermine particular individuals and their performances. As with any successful performance, timing is crucial, and the viewing audience are likely to be more conscious of 'dead air' (stumbles and pauses, mis-cues and breaths) from the ordinary person, revealing how much the apparently ordinary improvised talk of professionals is, in fact, carefully timed and scripted. However, sympathy is not always guaranteed for contestants by a good performance as if they were professionals. One of the most common observations concerning *Blind Date* relates to the unacknowledged, practised nature of the contestant's apparently spontaneous responses, which is often articulated by viewers as dissatisfaction or displeasure, relating to an absence of looked for naturalness in these moments and, more generally, from the ordinary person. The framing of the natural or ordinary individual must therefore be carefully managed in order to please an audience suspicious of a too obviously practised charm but nevertheless enamoured of both naïve or natural candour and the activities of the real eccentric.

The eccentric is, of course, an extreme representative of the ordinary person who is liberated rather than constrained by the television medium. This individual either satisfactorily conceals his sophisticated understanding of the television audience or is ignorant of their expectations. He or she may appear to the watching audience as a natural, as an original (literally extraordinary), and may be accompanied by strange pets, or simply manifest bizarre skills, mannerisms, unusual accents, and/or opinions. In the appropriate context (in shows such as *That's Life!* or *Barrymore*) although they may be extreme, these ordinary people are still not 'performing'— the audience believes (or wants to believe) that they *are* characters, extroverts discovered by the researcher and, eventually, the camera. Ultimately, the audience does not want the ordinary individual to be too polished—a too professional amateur may be read as pushy, embarrassing, or desperate for fame. A too naked desire for celebrity on the part of the ordinary person may, in fact, be dangerous. As I have observed in an earlier chapter, the notorious activities of the 'The Hopefuls' on Channel 4's *The Word* demonstrate how the viewer's distaste can resolve itself as sadistic pleasure, as the ordinary person is punished or humiliated for his or her unseemly desire to perform.

The television audience may be anxious (and occasionally antagonistic) about ordinary people as performers for at least two reasons. Firstly, the otherwise accepted duality of character and actor is made problematic when we witness real people perform. For if real people convincingly 'put on an act' where can sincerity, authenticity, and real emotion be located with any conviction? The collapse of the distinction between appearance and actuality does not need to be intellectualized to become a focus for legitimate concern. While acting may be pleasurable when we know we are watching a performance (it is, after all, a 'skilful' activity), when an ordinary performer acts, we may become uncomfortably aware of how appearance and reality (the behaviour and the feelings) of the performer may be no more matched in everyday life than they are on screen.

Secondly, the audience may simply feel that ordinary people are being forced to perform, coerced into making a fool of themselves, and that their presence or image on screen has been manipulated by technicians, producers, and bullying presenters. In other words, we empathize uncomfortably with their lack of control. There is therefore often an uneasy ambivalence in the appreciation of the ordinary person. On the one hand we may anticipate disaster, and while we may (carefully framed) enjoy this, on the other hand we may also be pleasantly surprised when the ordinary person wins, not just by giving the right answers but when he or she effectively 'takes control' of either the technology (the camcorder or the interviewer's microphone) or the performance context itself (that is the studio, the emotional and intellectual agenda).

The relationship between a yoof television presenter and the ordinary person often highlights the ambivalence arising through the mixture of pleasure and anxiety felt by the audience in relation to the performance or presence of the ordinary individual. The characteristics the yoof television presenter often bring into the foreground are both a hoped-for spontaneity, as well as the less comfortable concept of unpredictability associated with the interaction between host and ordinary individual—as we will see in two specific incidents from Chris Evans's career.

In general, the characteristic style of the yoof television presenter is marked by the loss of any distinction between the public and the private and a characteristic self-reflexivity. This is associated with a kind of knowingness on the part of the presenter/host that ultimately reveals itself, almost exclusively, as a form of television literacy. Literacy, in this sense, may be understood to be the ability to play with and parody various genres and conventions. Both Dominik Diamond and Richard O' Brien, whom I discussed in detail in the last chapter, manifest this style, but it is also evident to a greater or lesser extent in the performances of other presenters, such as, for example, Jonathan Ross (presenting the *Last Resort*), Johnny Vaughan (*MovieWatch* and latterly *The Big Breakfast*), Katie Puckrik (initially of *The Word*), and Antoine de Caunes (*Rapido*, *Eurotrash*). However, the most successful proponent of this kind of performance has to be Chris Evans, who now presents and produces *TFI Friday*, having worked earlier on *The Big Breakfast* and his own *Don't Forget Your Toothbrush*.

Although his performance has developed over a period of years, Evans's style brings together all the significant aspects of this particular mode of presentation. Firstly, his vocal delivery is extremely fast so that the pace of the programme is rapid and urgent; the viewer is obliged to keep up with Evans or simply marvel at his vocal dexterity and persistence. Secondly, his linguistic style is also dependent on the repetition of phrases with slightly varying intonation. For example, in the earlier game show, *Don't Forget Your Toothbrush*, Evans reappears after the commercial break and claims—'I'm losing my voice . . . the voice is going . . . I *am* lo*sing* my voice.' The effect of this is that Evans can be seen to be 'milking' his predicament to the extent that it becomes part of the show rather than a disruption. In addition, because of the way Evans is confident enough apparently to work without his script, it appears that he is improvising. This is a feature that is also emphasized by the way in which he may add comments or observations about his script as he goes along—with asides such as 'that didn't work', 'it worked in rehearsal', and so forth. Thirdly, Evans uses other people, co-presenters, the crew, the studio audience, ordinary performers, even technology itself to bolster and structure his performance. He therefore employs the 'Zoo' mode of presentation I discussed in the second chapter. His behaviour with these external 'props' is playful, even boyish. For the most part their purpose seems to suggest that Evans's direct address to camera should not be seen as a monologue, but as a form of speech that is more akin to a dialogic triangle in which the viewer also seemingly takes part. This is also encouraged by the way in which Evans spends a lot of his time making sure that the audience at home feels included. In *Don't Forget Your Toothbrush* (hereafter *DFYTB*), although Evans asks for, and receives, confirmation and reactions from the studio audience (and from regular co-performers such as Jools Holland[2]), he also pays particular attention to the watching viewer. In particular, Evans frequently employs a viewer-specific device to link sections of *DFYTB*. In one programme a pattern of drumbeats is cued on the soundtrack, and Evans turns from camera to camera, presenting his profile and then a wide-eyed stare down the barrel of the appropriate lens; and, of course, vision is cut from camera to camera in perfect synch with his movements. To the studio audience all this means little or nothing; to the viewer at home, it provides an amusing punctuation to the programme's flow of events and a display of virtuosity on Evans's part. While such techniques reveal an apparently boyish enthusiasm for the technology, this specific link also generates a brief inter-textual moment. On the one hand, it is an aside to those moments when other studio presenters—all too frequently—deliver portentous pieces to camera to the wrong camera entirely. On the other hand, the inter-textual nature of the sequence was due to the fact that this little bit of camera play was also clearly a homage to the (cult) children's puppet programme *Captain Scarlet and The Mysterons*. The distinctive drum beat, in combination with the rapid cutting between alternate perspectives was a particular hallmark of *Captain Scarlet*, which used such sequences (like Evans) to make the transition between different scenes in the programme. This is a direct appeal to the cult sensibilities of Generation X, as it is both about television itself and about an experience of television at a particular time. For whilst *Captain Scarlet* was originally transmitted in the late 1960s it was repeated

---

2 Jools Holland is, like Paula Yates, an ex-presenter of *The Tube* and known previously as part of the band Squeeze.

during the 1970s—the decade when many of the target audience would have been children.[3]

Another way in which Evans appears to privilege the home audience can be seen in the way that he will create an apparently intimate link between his performance and the watching audience, pulling them in to particular moments of tension or interest. In one episode of *DFYTB* (the first of the second series) Evans sets up a surprise/game which involves a young woman's most treasured possession (a battered teddy bear, called Long Legs) being suspended, a hundred feet up, over the Thames river. Evans describes, with the assistance of home photos, the sentimental attachment the woman has for the bear and then asks her (Margo) whether or not she would be willing to drop the bear in the water for one thousand pounds. Unsurprisingly, this particular challenge involves the rowdy participation of the rest of the studio audience and Evans expends some energy as he scurries around in an attempt to garner some consensus. He also spends a lot of time talking directly to the camera and presents various nods of affirmation, or negation, as well as grimaces of despair, away from the audience and directly into the lens of the camera, as if he were saving his 'real feelings' for the viewing audience alone.[4] As it stands, this particular sequence may not appear to be that different from the dilemmas that are set up within the relatively conventional formats of similar programmes such as *Noel's House Party* or *Surprise, Surprise*. What is distinctive is the way in which Evans fails (or simply does not want) to establish an empathetic relationship between the viewer at home and Margo, the ordinary person plucked from the studio audience. At one point, for example, he says to Margo—who appears to be confronting a genuine dilemma—'My heart is breaking for you.' Almost in the same breath, Evans turns to the camera to shake his head violently and whisper 'no it isn't'.

There are other factors that make this sequence peculiarly uncomfortable and ambivalent. One of these is that the thousand pounds is visible, displayed in a suitcase, which is held open by the hostess as close as possible to Margo who remains seated in the audience; this ensures that the exchange appears particularly vulgar. Another disquieting element is that Margo appears genuinely upset, and, as Evans observes, she is clearly 'welling up'. In fact, when she does make the decision to 'drop the teddy' she seems to be sincerely distressed, and is comforted by her mother who is sitting next to her (and who, ironically, must have been 'in' on the scheme in the first place). Evans exacerbates the discomfort of the viewing audience as he is unwilling

3 It was also repeated in the late 1980s in the youth schedule of BBC2—between 6 and 7.30 p.m. on weekdays.

4 In some senses this is not dissimilar to the arch performance of Richard O'Brien in *The Crystal Maze*.

to make it clear which decision she should make. At one point, for example, he comments, 'You didn't have a thousand pounds before you came here tonight so it won't make any difference to your life if you go home without it'; an observation not generally made by game show hosts, who usually rely on the hope that contestants 'have enjoyed themselves', even if (or when) they are not successful.[5] In addition to this, Evans seems to assume that the audience at home are callous enough to feel that Margo should rush to make her decision; as she hesitates, he comments: 'Yes, or no? She said yes once, but then she said no straightaway, so we've got to stick with it viewers, I'm sorry about that, commercials will be soon.' It is this last comment, along with Evans's frequent mugging to camera, which suggests that there is clearly meant to be no real empathy with Margo's moral dilemma; it is revealed instead as a timed spectacle that, if Evans is not careful, may threaten to exceed its limits. Evans's dismissive attitude towards Margo is also confirmed by the way in which, once Margo makes her decision, he tosses away his prompt card—and therefore his notes concerning her relationship to her teddy—and excitedly declares 'It was all lies.' Obviously, this suggests that the viewer must not take it seriously, which is surprisingly difficult when observing what appears to be Margo's genuine distress. Ultimately, of course, this is also justified by the fact that it is revealed that Long Legs will be rescued—'I promise . . . I hope', claims Evans—and the teddy is indeed retrieved to be reunited with Margo later in the show.[6]

Yet Evans's continually cavalier use of the ordinary person is also demonstrated by several items on *TFI Friday*, particularly 'Freak or Unique' and 'Ugly Bloke'. In 'Freak or Unique' apparently ordinary people demonstrate skills or body manipulation that veer from the banal to the truly disgusting; a less sadistic version of 'The Hopefuls', the purpose is pure voyeurism. In the item 'Ugly Bloke' a less than attractive male is given the opportunity to 'turn down' a beautiful woman. Despite the fact the ugly bloke is apparently a volunteer it is difficult to determine whether the audience is being asked to participate in the equally cynical pleasures of either gawking at the ugly guy, or supposedly supporting him in his opportunity apparently to humiliate the beautiful woman. Neither position offers any point of sincere connection, and somehow this is precisely the point. It is not a real encounter, and the audience knows that the woman is being paid and not truly humiliated, and they are supported in their voyeuristic distaste towards the 'ugly bloke' as he is apparently willing to be identified as such.

5 Recently, however, Chris Tarrant has often used this nudge to hesitant contestants on the unashamedly vulgar *Who Wants To Be a Millionaire?*

6 Despite Long Legs's retrieval this particular incident caused a record number of complaints to Channel 4.

Evans's attitude towards the 'ordinary person' is therefore ambivalent. This applies both to the ordinary person on-screen and occasionally to the ordinary viewer at home. In one episode of *TFI Friday*, it is the viewers at home he teases, rather than a member of the public who has volunteered (or, like Margo, one of an apparently unsuspecting studio audience). Yet, like his antics in *DFYTB*, his play with the viewer at home is mediated through a play with the visual and aural aspects of the television medium. Claiming to have been a television viewer himself the previous week, and thus justifying his view that *TFI Friday* is a 'godsend' of a show—as he has now seen that there is nothing else on—Evans decides deliberately to tease part of his television audience by employing visual graphics to confuse the viewer who has either tuned in late, or who may be otherwise distracted. Firstly, he calls for an 'ickle 4' to be placed in the corner of the screen, thus attempting to reproduce the channel number which often appears on the television monitor when using the remote control.[7] Joking with his on-screen audience Evans then rubs his hands in glee claiming that the viewer will now be desperately trying to remove the 4. To exacerbate their supposed confusion he then asks for a volume indicator to appear horizontally across the bottom of the screen. He then proceeds to order that the sound be turned down so that nothing can be heard. There then follows two or three minutes of vision only where Evans appears to be having some animated conversations with his on-screen crowd. This is not as radical as it seems, however, as this dead air is shortly filled by a voice-over who begins by commiserating with the watching viewer and then inviting them to send for tickets to attend the show in person. Why would Evans risk alienating his viewing audience like this? The answer is, of course, because it is not actually about alienating the viewer, but rather works to support Evans's pose as a cheeky 'ordinary' punter who, like the home audience, is familiar with the 'other side' of the screen. Evans, it appears, may be a celebrity but he watches television, and plays with his remote control just like the viewer at home. Though part of the audience may be confused by his antics they will, crucially, be the latecomer, the disinterested, or the distracted viewer. They will not be the viewers who have been watching closely since the show began; for these more faithful or ideal viewers Evans's antics will actually be inclusive. They will get the 'joke' whereas everyone else may not.[8]

In this way Evans offers himself as a conduit between the world of television and the celebrity and that of the ordinary person, or viewer

7 *TFI Friday* is shown on Channel 4 in the UK.

8 If the event is really an attempt to confuse the viewer it is pretty poor. Evans announces each change he is about to make, and as I have indicated, there are both visual and aural cues that reveal that something is afoot—namely the volume graphic on screen and the voice over.

at home. Occasionally, however, this pose fails. In an interview with Mariella Frostrup (a female television presenter) Evans encourages her to talk about their shared neighbourhood, and jokes with her about the joys of putting out their bins and catching glimpses of their famous neighbours. Here Evans appears to be both of, and separate to, the world he inhabits; for while wealthy enough to live in such an exclusive neighbourhood he is, apparently, like the ordinary viewer, still star struck. Then, however, Mariella good-naturedly teases him about his failure to attend a recent party she held. It appears that he initially could not have made it because he was to have interviewed Prince, the rock star; this having fallen through, Mariella teases him, claiming that he failed to show up because he was scared that Penny Smith (another presenter and news-reader) might be attending. Penny Smith is an attractive blonde, and, as many viewers would know, is exactly Evans's 'type' of woman—all of his girlfriends and his ex-wife are blonde. Yet Evans's hasty interruption 'Let's leave Penny Smith out of this' confirms that something has gone awry. This instance is revealing as his refusal to allow any follow up on this demonstrates the limits to Evans's apparent willingness to present his private self, for it is certainly a revelation or comment that if it had been about the celebrity guest he would have made them elaborate. Evans's persona therefore negotiates a fine line: while he wants to offer the viewer access to his lifestyle celebrating it as one of the 'rich and famous' and demonstrating the pleasures of being 'on television', he also needs to protect his private self, and carefully maintain his air of not taking it all too seriously. Real emotions and sensibilities therefore remain off limits. In addition as an ordinary bloke he must not be seen to invest too heavily in a world that is beyond most of his viewers; for while they may be fascinated with the gossip and glamour of the celebrity lifestyle they are also deeply sceptical of its worth.

Evans has a particular status within the yoof genre. As a post-modern performer he articulates a tone of moral ambivalence. In his universe there are no right or wrong answers; simply a spectacle that does, or does not work. The visual excess generated within *TFI Friday* and *DFYTB*, whether this is in the former through garish graphics, a busy *mise en scène*, and roving cameras, or in the latter though Evans's costume of loud suits, along with the garish set and hectic camera work, make his shows variations on a spectacle that parodies those other programmes which surprise ordinary people and/or publicly reveal their supposedly illicit behaviour. In both shows he walks an uneasy line between celebrating and humiliating the ordinary individual. Yet his performances and shows are not really about subverting the genre but celebrating and exceeding its limits. He is a performer whose very style and persona is marked by his intimacy, and enchantment, with television. He is consistently reflexive about his role as a television presenter (as someone who is 'on' television) and, increasingly, self-reflexive about himself, though his allusions as to how much he earns and who he fancies are in fact much more guarded than they might, at first, appear. Yet because he also lays claim to ordinary experiences—puerile jokes, hangovers, evenings watching television—Evans can play his roles as though they were in quotation marks; he is a 'game show host', a 'television presenter' with all the self-consciousness this implies. As his performance has developed (and this is particularly marked in *TFI Friday*) there is also increasingly a sense in which his behaviour is emptied of meaning; the real self that is (apparently) Chris Evans is supposedly as public as the self that is the 'presenter'. As Evans demonstrates at the end of the first run of *TFI Friday* it is as appropriate for Evans to host the show from his own home (taking the show with him) as it is to present it from the studios in Riverside. Everything about Evans, then, appears to be in the foreground; rarely, if ever, self-effacing, he presents himself as much as the programmes he performs in.

Evans's success with Generation X is not surprising: his references —old and current television programmes, football games and heroes, musical tastes—appear to be the same as theirs. He demonstrates this both through his choice of guests but also in the phrases he uses, his gestures, and in the content of his speech. His mode of performance is at once both conventional and excessive, allowing him to do his job but appear to be 'faking it'. Evans can appear fascinated, even excited by the world he inhabits, but never sincere, for sincerity is no longer necessarily prized, or even understood in the way it might once have been. The explosion of media focused solely on the most banal aspects of celebrities' lives—in magazines such as *Hello!* and *Now*—and the increasingly high profile of media managers (whether it be public relations, or advertising and promotions) means that contemporary audiences are particularly aware of the way in which personalities can be manipulated, and the various ways in which they can be constructed as 'genuine', as 'sincere' or 'natural'. The revelations given by celebrities on chat shows have long since been understood to be circumspect and often contrived, and displays of real emotion by ordinary people (or by the famous) are no longer special and even arouse a certain amount of suspicion in the audience. As Andrew Tolson suggests:

> Even when interviewees are apparently 'being themselves' we can never know whether or not to take them seriously. The talk show has become a game, and 'personality' is now demonstrated by a willingness to play; not by revealing all, with apparent sincerity, in a televised confession.[9]

---

9 Andrew Tolson, *Mediations: Text and Discourse in Media Studies* (London: Edward Arnold, 1996), 149.

In these circumstances, what Evans suggests in his performance is that it is now appropriate to behave as if nothing matters except playing the game. In this instance, television performance is no longer a tool that demonstrates or calls up a range of emotions, and which is designed to interest and engage the viewer; instead, performance begins to be dominated by spectacle, and Evans works hard to make a spectacle of himself and others. Yet he does so in a typically ambivalent manner appropriate to Generation X; his excess and blatant insincerity seem to imply a degree of cynicism about this kind of behaviour and the world he inhabits. Yet his mode of address and his excitability demonstrate his enchantment with television and his own celebrity. Evans, like his audience, grew up with television, understands it, and is seduced, yet he apparently recognizes it as a game played too often and thus relies on a core of cynicism to prevent him from becoming another dupe in relation to television's putative glamour and power.

All performers and performances demonstrate or reveal some aspects of the wider culture; post-modern performers such as Evans reflect many of the anxieties and concerns experienced by Generation X. For in their performances they demonstrate, and articulate, a way of both revelling in, and sneering at, the world of celebrities and television itself.

6

Conclusions
The Viewing Experience

The empire of the habitual is the matrix of mental and social
life, made of mundane opportunities and choices and composed of practices conducted half-aware, which assemble one's
very personhood. What is new in contemporary life are not
these institutions of mobile privatization per se but the interpenetration of layer upon layer of built environment and
representation, the formative and the derivative, the imaginary
and the mundane.[1]

THOUGH the focus of my study has been relatively narrow—
British youth programmes from the late 1980s and early 1990s
—there has also been a wider-ranging discussion concerned
to illustrate a particular viewing sensibility. While I argue that it is
symptomatic of a particular generation of viewers (who were young
between 1987 and 1995), it does not, of course, reflect every one of
those young viewers' experiences of television. This apparent lack of
fit is justified by the way in which youth in this study is not determined by age, but relates to a historical and mediated construction
of 'youth' or 'youthfulness' as an attitude, or a series of traits, habits,
and beliefs. However, as a kind of viewing experience, youth as 'yoof'
remains specific, and of its time, in at least one sense. I think 'yoof'
television and its viewers must be understood to be one possible
response to the kind of environment that Margaret Morse describes
in the extract I use to introduce this chapter. Here, Morse is suggesting that we are increasingly subject to a world where we are part of
'the interpenetration of layer upon layer of built environment and
representation, the formative and the derivative, the imaginary and
the mundane'. This mix of the past with the present, the inauthentic
with the real, the banal with the fantastic, is clearly a post-modern
environment. The programmes I have examined are clearly a response
to, and, to a certain extent, a reflection of, this same environment.

---

1 Margaret Morse, 'An Ontology of Everyday Distraction: The Freeway, the Mall, and
Television', in Patricia Mellencamp (ed.), *Logics of Television: Essays in Cultural
Criticism* (London: British Film Institute, 1990), 210.

There seems to be little escape from post-modernism, even though it was clear fairly early on in its application to television studies that its easy fit in relation to theories about television was deceptive. Specifically, it was John Fiske's book, *Television Culture*,[2] that was seen by many critics as an unfortunate over-extension, and a mistaken interpretation of some aspects of post-modernism—in particular in its celebration of polysemy, contradiction, and his incautious promotion of the openness of the television text. Fiske's detailed discussions elaborating the ways in which television texts might be seen to be necessarily inter-textual and therefore open to a wide variety of divergent readings, and his validation of pleasure as a form of resistance, attracted many critics. A recent attack appears in Richard Dienst's book, *Still Life in Real Time*. Here Dienst satirizes Fiske's approach by adapting the occasionally evangelical tone of the latter's writing:

> Television reveals itself as a curiosity shop that viewers enter and leave at will, rummaging through textual shards for delights and perhaps edification. Their task is eased by the co-operation of the texts, which offer themselves—through the weak links of flow— as rich morsels of indeterminate meaning, waiting to be brought home and blended into each viewer's polysemic, kaleidoscopic experience.[3]

And I, too, would want to distinguish my approach from Fiske's, although I have also been concerned to illustrate how it is possible for the viewer to make more than one kind of sense out of any individual programme text. Yet, instead of attempting to illustrate the potential for many readings by many viewers, I have been more interested in developing a profile of a viewing experience that seems to me to be repeatedly interpellated (called on and defined) by a series of designated programme texts. So, although I have been rather free with the concept of post-modernism and used it as a way of defining a sensibility, a historical and social context, and even as a way of performing, I would not argue that it be universally applied to all the possible experiences of television, or to the textual strategies of many television programmes. Yet in the case of the programmes I have described, it does seem that post-modernism suggests a fit between a particular social context, an identity, and a developing aesthetic strategy. In particular it is post-modernism's embrace of ambivalence, which suggests that it is a useful way in which to think about these texts' balance between cynicism *and* enchantment. Programmes like *Network 7, The Word, TFI Friday*, and *MTV's Most Wanted* display formal strategies

2 John Fiske, *Television Culture* (London: Routledge, 1987).

3 Richard Dienst, *Still Life in Real Time: Theory after Television* (Durham, NC, and London: Duke University Press, 1994), 31.

that are clearly contradictory, unless they are understood to appeal to viewers who enjoy watching television, who know a great deal about the mechanics and techniques of making programmes, but who have become cynical about the illusions they engineer, and who are therefore uneasy about their own relationship with the medium as a whole.

What I have tried to do is to provide a nuanced, and specific, analysis of a shift in the viewing experiences of part of the television audience. It is a mode of viewing that has, since the start of my study, gained some popular currency. Here, for example, is Douglas Rushkoff, celebrating something akin to the sensibility I have attempted to describe, although this time in relation to American audiences:

> I go on to give my rap on TV: people with remote controls are less willing to be pulled into the programming trance. They will increasingly prefer shows like *Seinfield* or *Beavis and Butthead* that have distancing devices built in.[4]

Yet many popular critics forget the persistence of other ways of seeing and experiencing media texts, of enjoying them, and submitting to the pleasures they provide. As I suggested in my initial chapter, it is important to remember that many soap operas such as *Neighbours*, *Brookside*, and *Eastenders* are watched avidly by many of the same viewers who watched Chris Evans's antics on *The Big Breakfast*. Although it could be argued that soaps can also be read ironically—an approach in which viewers bring along their own 'distancing devices'—I do not believe that the long-term emotional and cognitive investment that these soaps demand can be entirely sustained by such a viewing perspective. Instead, the evidence I have provided should fit into a wider perspective, where, as Jim Collins claims, postmodernism can be understood to suggest a context where many styles—and identities, as well as modes of viewing—can be seen to coexist simultaneously. My feeling is that the current experience of television is distinguished by the co-presence of many different ways of seeing. This is something similar to the argument Kevin Robins presents in his article 'Will Images Move Us Still?' where, basing his thoughts on a previous argument by David Phillips, he suggests:

> Against the idea of a sequential narrative of succeeding image cultures, and against the narrative logic of successive narrative breaks, Phillips argues that 'vision operates instead as a palimpsest which conflates many different modes of perception—a model which applies both to the history of vision and to the perception of a singular observer'. This seems to me a very productive metaphor . . . Rather than privileging 'new' against

---

4 Douglas Rushkoff, 'On the Guess List', *Guardian*, 16 Jan. 1997, 7 (on-line supplement).

'old' images, we might then think about them all—all those that are still active, at least—in their contemporaneity. From such a perspective, what is significant is precisely the multiplicity and diversity of contemporary images.[5]

In accordance with this, some of my arguments suggest that young viewers may relate to television in ways that include both old and new ways of dealing with the 'diversity and multiplicity of contemporary images'. For example, several of the viewing tactics that I have described—the 'reading around the screen', the understanding of *mise en scène* as a collage or 'pin-board'—relate to older and coexistent media habits, such as young people's ability to read, and make sense of, a magazine such as *Smash Hits* or *i-D*, or in the construction of their own media-informed *mise en scène* in a bedroom populated by posters, postcards, and photographs. What I have implied is that such tactics coexist with, and supplement, newer relations to the text that are generated by visual technologies such as the computer, and the computer game.

In my introductory chapter I made it clear that my use of postmodernism is not intended to suggest a break, or a radical and universal change, in the experience of viewing. Rather, it relates closely to different factors at work within a post-modern economic and social context. This includes the proliferation of media, the pervasiveness of the commodity, and the increasing instability of life and career structures. This has led to the production of a series of texts which speak to, and attempt to define, a generation of television viewers who understand that they are part of a culture in which it is increasingly difficult to pursue an identity that is recognizably unified and consistent. It is also apparent that this inconsistency of self is being policed by a continually self-reflexive impulse; the purpose of this impulse is constantly to check any naïve (or unqualified) investment in places and people that may all too easily be revealed as temporary, fake, or deceptive. This investment or long-term engagement with things or with people has become increasingly problematic as a culture has developed in which the individual understands that it has become difficult and potentially irrelevant to distinguish between authentic and inauthentic practices and emotions.

This quality of self-reflexivity is the most obvious and the most consistent element of many of the programmes I have described. Although the self-reflexivity of many of the programmes may seem to imply a distancing between the viewer and text, I think that what my evidence suggests is that it may actually be a way of binding the viewer closer to the text. It reveals how the viewer can be (re)enchanted,

5 Kevin Robins, 'Will Images Move Us Still?', in M. Lister (ed.), *The Photographic Image in Digital Culture* (London and New York: Routledge, 1995), 45.

as self-reflexivity allows the programme to incorporate, without contradiction, and without a loss of coherence, various and even apparently conflicting sites for engagement (or ways of engaging) for the viewer. In fact, the self-reflexive aspects of the programme allow the viewer to oscillate between these different levels of investment. On the one hand, the inclusion of various performers, formats, and conventions may be done in a way that is clearly parodic or knowing; on the other hand, the reproduction of sites of unforgotten and familiar pleasures still appeals. Even the most knowing of viewers may be simultaneously charmed by the fantasy that is being reproduced within the text—whether this is the opportunity for a para-social relationship, the reconstruction of musical affect, or the materialization of a virtual world. Such fantasies are, in effect, sanctioned by the way in which the programme itself has (already) parodied or satirized them. The viewer is, in fact, all the more bewitched by the operations of the text, because there is little sense in which the satire or parody has any currency outwith the programme, or outside of television itself.

Such an analysis paints rather a bleak picture of an audience, who are, seemingly, duped by this form of programming, albeit in a sophisticated manner. However, it is also important to remember that not all television texts are like this, and that the viewing sensibility that these programmes articulate suggests that viewers are also able, as knowing individuals, to deconstruct other texts in an informed and sophisticated manner—a useful practice in an increasingly mediated environment. Yet this kind of negotiation can not imply or guarantee a resistance to the machinations of the media, and certainly not in any way that might be understood by critics looking for solutions to the problem of influence, or those who wish to determine a form of cultural resistance in the television audience. Those kinds of endeavour have not been the aim of this study; instead I have been more concerned to take a phenomenological approach to television, and to understand how it may take part in the 'identity-in-process' that was characteristic of Generation X.

I have not concerned myself with defending or criticizing the position of television in popular culture, rather, I wanted to illustrate the complexity of the relationship between the viewer and the medium in a way that avoided creating a totalizing theory or set of assumptions. Such generalizing, although it may be suggestive, often obscures the very specific nature of what it is, exactly, we are doing, when we 'watch television'. None the less, in the process of writing I have incorporated some wider observations about the viewing experience that both supplement and challenge various established assumptions and theories concerning television and its audience. In conclusion, therefore, I want to summarize and clarify what significance these observations could have in relation to a more general understanding of the television medium.

It has been confidently asserted by some critics that television produces within itself a 'perpetual present'—that is, a constant flow of images and sounds that are continually happening 'now', whether the viewer is there to witness it or not. This apparent absence of a past or process of remembering is then used to demonstrate that television must signal the destruction of popular and individual memory within society. Mary Ann Doane, in her article, 'Information, Crisis, Catastrophe', argues:

> Television . . . has been conceptualized as the annihilation of memory, and consequently of history, in its continual stress upon the 'nowness' of its own discourse. As Stephen Heath and Gillian Skirrow point out, 'where film sides towards instantaneous memory ('everything is absent, everything is *recorded*—as a memory trace which is so at once, without having been something else before'), television operates much more as an absence of memory, the recorded material it uses—including the material recorded image'.[6]

In a similar vein, Patricia Mellencamp, in her article 'TV Time and Catastrophe, or *Beyond the Pleasure Principle* of Television', draws on a reading of Walter Benjamin, and argues:

> TV is rarely the material object setting off involuntary (personal) memory, causing us to assimilate 'the information it supplies as part of [our] own experience.' 'Where there is experience in the strict sense of the word, certain contents of the individual past combine with material of the collective past.' Rather than this amalgam of involuntary/voluntary memory, shifting from conscious to unconscious, from collective to individual past in the realm of experience . . . television's 'intention is just the opposite, and it is achieved: to isolate what happens from the realm in which it could affect the experience of the reader.'[7]

The assumptions that lie behind these arguments imply that television insulates or isolates the viewer from the real world, or real experience. This is supported by the suggestion that television necessarily does this because it is unable to account for the passage of time—except, as both writers go on to suggest, in representation of the momentary interruptions caused by crisis and catastrophe. Mellencamp argues that this is related to the fact that what television does, after all, is to sell 'our' time; television's business is the occupation, usurpation, and commodification of the leisure time

---

6 Mary Ann Doane, 'Information, Crisis, Catastrophe', in Mellencamp (ed.), *Logics of Television*, 227.

7 Patricia Mellencamp, 'TV Time and Catastrophe, or *Beyond the Pleasure Principle* of Television', in Mellencamp (ed.), *Logics of Television*, 242.

of the viewer—which, in the first instance, of course, *belongs* to that viewer. She writes:

> US network television is a disciplinary time machine, a metronome rigorously apportioning the present, rerunning TV history, and anxiously awaiting the future. The hours, days, and television seasons are seriated, scheduled, and traded in ten-second increments modelled on the modern work week— day time, prime time, late night or weekend. Time itself is a gendered, hierarchized commodity, capitalizing on leisure.[8]

Television hides the (real) passage of time because it colonizes, packages, and sells the time of the viewer as if it were the property of television. In Mellencamp's analysis, it is as if television wants us to forget because it does not want the viewer to realize how much time he or she has wasted watching television; in other words, how much time television has, in effect, stolen from the viewer. As Mellencamp develops her argument, television becomes pathological: it 'reruns and remakes', she says, 'Freud's "repetition compulsion."'[9] These arguments suggest that television can only produce a faulty, unreliable, or unevocative series of memories; television, Mellencamp claims, can only schedule 'memories of television'. It is therefore unable to provide what she identifies as the 'amalgam of involuntary/ voluntary memory', that is, in Proustian terms, a situation where a sensual experience can trigger, involuntarily, a series of remembered instances that urge the individual, voluntarily, to recall and reflect upon personal experience. Television, she suggests, thus fails to call up this amalgam that can speak of, or construct, a sense of who and where you are now (understood as opposed to the person you were, then and there). My argument, in contrast, has suggested that television may in fact have begun to take a part in this process.

What lies at the basis of Doane's and Mellencamp's arguments is what has often been understood to be the definitive characteristic of the television experience; this is the concept of 'flow' first theorized by Raymond Williams in his book *Television: Technology and Cultural Form*. Flow can be understood to function at various different levels in relation to the television medium. At one level, flow (and therefore experience of television as flow) is a way of conceiving the series of programme texts (the programmes, the station idents and programme menus, the advertisements and continuity announcements) as continuous and related to one another. This occurs in ways that are both overt—designated by the organization of the published schedule—and covert—in the relationship between the advertise-

---

8 Ibid., 240.
9 Ibid., 241.

ments and the programmes, and in the timely 'interruption' of trailers into programme breaks. In this way it is possible to see how

> television survives through flow, whose transmission washes away the particularity of its messages along with the differences between them, and whose reception drains perception of its resistant holding powers of distance and memory. Thus flow absorbs the entirety of the televisual textual process.[10]

Yet it is important to remember that flow also relates to the behaviour or the viewing process of the television audience, who, I have suggested, are often busy in the process of setting their own course in the 'stream' of televisual images and sounds, or programmes and programming fragments. The absence of this audience is, in part, what I find problematic about Mellencamp and Doane's arguments. For, to follow the logic of their suggestions, televisual flow would necessarily be understood to dominate the perceptual activities of the audience. In effect, if television is necessarily forgetful, so too, apparently, is the audience. Mellencamp, for instance, directly states that television cannot be the 'material object' that can evoke personal memory. In contrast to this, what I have suggested throughout is that to understand television, to engage with the particular televisual aesthetic outlined here, Generation X had to remember; it had to have learnt from television. Television was meaningful in many instances because of the way that it interacted with memory. This is because for these viewers (and myself, I suppose) television is part of their experience of being in the world, it has always been more than a machine that represents an experience that is, somehow, 'elsewhere' to the experience of television itself.

Perhaps the best way that I can illustrate what I mean by television being 'part of their experience' is to suggest how far we have come from previous conceptions of how television engages its audience. Here is John Ellis, in his book *Visible Fictions*, discussing the way in which the televisual 'look at the world' substitutes itself for the look of the television viewer:

> Broadcast TV recruits the interest of its viewers by creating a complicity of viewing: the TV look at the world becomes a surrogate look for the viewers. TV presents the events of the world, both documented and imagined, to an audience that is secure at home, relaxing and seeking diversion. Broadcast TV creates a community of address in which viewer and TV institution both look at a world that exists beyond them both.[11]

10 Dienst, *Still Life in Real Time*, 33.

11 John Ellis, *Visible Fictions: Cinema, Television, Video* (London: Routledge, 1982; revised edn., 1992), 163.

I think that it is now very difficult to sustain the idea that television is separate either from the rest of the world, or from the world of the viewer. The point is, surely, that its presence has increased the permeability between these different worlds. If this is even only partially the case, or only true for some viewers, television can, nevertheless, still be understood (to employ another concept originated by Raymond Williams) to form part of the 'structure of feeling' that is experienced by individuals in their everyday lives. This means that television has to be a material factor in the way that people behave, remember, or simply feel themselves to be part of contemporary life.

Yoof television, I suggest, was the televisual aesthetic which emerged in the attempt to articulate this new relationship. It revealed that a particular kind of sensibility or sensate knowledge was at work. Using terms such as sensibility and knowledge should indicate the tactile, experiential elements that inform this mode of television viewing. Yet while encroaching and cumulative, it was also contradictory. While the increasing familiarity with the medium made the viewer aware of the forms of television in a way that encouraged a distancing, or critical detachment from television programmes, at the same time the visceral nature of the experienced (the everyday) viewer's relationship with television conversely revealed how bound in the viewer was to the medium. The fact of 'being experienced' was in itself evidence of the way in which the viewer must have been caught up in, and engaged with, television over time and within specific contexts. Thus a knowledge of television both pulls the viewer away from, and yet also reveals how he or she is pulled back into, the text. This contradiction is maintained by a successful incorporation of both cynicism and enchantment—a mixture of wariness and enthusiasm. It has been my argument that this is indeed what links and distinguishes this youth audience—Generation X—and many of the programme texts that attempted to address their specific concerns.

In the future, this sensibility may seem as redundant as the conception of the 'passive' viewer. The real, as opposed to the speculative, effects of the multi-channel experience, or the actual affect of the (as yet, imperfectly realized) interactive potential of new media technologies will, necessarily, inspire other patterns of viewing and other ways of relating to the media forms that now play such a fundamental part in our lives.

As the generation who were once 'yoof' ages, it is possible to see how the sensibility I have described has now entered the mainstream —no longer 'yoof' but 'entertainment'. Indeed, the BBC's Youth department has long been swallowed up by Entertainment. Sankha Guha from *Network 7* and *The Rough Guide* presents items on the placid *Holiday*, and Gaby Roslin fills in for the late Jill Dando on the BBC's millennium night special. Chris Evans has successfully sold his media company—The Ginger Group—yet *TFI Friday* is struggling to keep viewers. But traces remain; one notable success is the Sunday morning schedule on Channel 4. Called 'T4' it has a familiar, but engaging, mix of ironic cartoon shows and imported and domestic teen soaps. On the BBC, running in the old Def II slot from 6 p.m. to 7.30 p.m. on BBC2, cult science-fiction shows and reruns of *The Simpsons* offer their own diluted version of cynicism and enchantment. Yet *The Simpsons* also appears in the Saturday morning children's magazine show *Live and Kicking*. *The Simpsons'* apparent ability to appeal to diverse audiences is not surprising; for, like the yoof audience they appeal to, Bart and his family are eminently adaptable and can be employed in a variety of ways. The difference, of course, is that Bart—the paradigmatic post-modern kid—never grew up.

Television Programmes

Youth Programmes

The Big Breakfast (C4/Planet 24, 1992–).
The Chartshow (cont. as) *The ITV Chartshow* (ITV/Video Visuals, 1986–98).
Crystal Maze (C4/Chatsworth TV, 1990–).
Don't Forget Your Toothbrush I & II (C4/Ginger Productions, 1994, 1995).
Eurotrash (C4/Rapido TV, 1993–).
Fantasy Football League (BBC2/Avalon-Grandslam, *c*.1994–6).
Gamesmaster (C4/Hewland International, 1992–5).
The Hitman and Her (ITV/Granada, *c*.1988–92).
Last Resort (C4/Callender Co./Channel X, 1987–8).
The Living Soap (BBC, 1993–4).
Moviewatch (C4/Chapter One Productions, 1993–).
Network 7 (C4/ Sunday Productions, 1987, 1988).
Never Mind the Buzzcocks (BBC/Talkback, 1996–).
Oh Boy! (ABC TV, 1958–9).
Passengers (C4/Rapido TV, 1994–5).
Rapido (BBC2, 1988–92).
Ready Steady Go (A-R, 1963–6).
Rough Guide to the . . . (BBC2, 1988–92).
Shooting Stars (BBC/Channel X, 1995, 1996, 1997).
Six-Five Special (BBC-TV, 1957–8).
Snub TV (BBC2 Snub TV, *c*.1987–90).
TFI Friday (C4/Ginger Productions, 1996–).
Takeover TV (C4 / World of Wonder, 1995–6).
Teenage Diaries (BBC2, 1992–3).
Top of the Pops (BBC1, 1964–).
The Tube (C4/Tyne Tees TV, 1982–7).
The White Room (C4/Initial Film and TV, 1995–6).
The Word (C4/24hr Productions, 1990–1; C4/Planet 24, 1991–5).
The Word: Access All Areas (C4/Planet 24, 1992–3).

General Programmes

Barrymoore (ITV/LWT, 1991–).
Blankety-Blank (BBC1, 1979–).
Blind Date (ITV/LWT, 1985–).
Brookside (C4/Brookside productions, 1982–).
Captain Scarlet and the Mysterons (ITC/ 21 Century Productions, 1967–8).
Eastenders (BBC1, 1985–).
The Generation Game (BBC1, 1971–).
Gladiators (LWT, 1992–).
Good morning with Anne and Nick (BBC1, 1992–6).

The Krypton Factor (Granada TV, 1977–93).
Later . . . with Jools Holland (BBC2, 1992–).
Life on Earth (BBC2, 1979).
Live and Kicking (BBC, 1993–).
Mastermind (BBC1, 1972–97).
Men Behaving Badly (Thames TV/ Hartswood Films, 1992; BBC1/Hartswood Films, 1992–8).
Neighbours (Grundy TV; on BBC1 since 1986).
Newsnight (BBC2, 1980–).
Noel's House Party (BBC1, 1991–9).
Question Time (BBC1, 1979–).
The Sky at Night (BBC, 1957–).
Surprise, Surprise (LWT, 1984–).
That's Life! (BBC1, 1973–94).
They Think It's All Over (BBC1/Talkback Productions, 1995–).
This Morning (Granada, 1988–).
Three of a Kind (BBC1, 1981, 1983).
University Challenge (BBC2, Granada, 1994–).
Vanessa (BBC1, 1999).
Video Nation (BBC, 1994–6).
What's Up Doc? (ITV/TVS, 1992–3; ITV/STV, 1993–5).
Who Wants To Be a Millionaire? (Celdaor, 1999–).

Bibliography

ADORNO, THEODOR, and HORKHEIMER, MAX, 'The Culture Industry: Enlightenment as Mass Deception', repr. in T. W. Adorno, *The Culture Industry: Selected Essays on Mass Culture*, ed. J. M. Bernstein (London: Routledge, 1991).

ALLEN, ROBERT C. (ed.), *Channels of Discourse, Reassembled: Television and Contemporary Criticism* (London and New York: Routledge, 1988).

ARMSTRONG, STEPHEN, 'Yoof's Rebel Rousers', *Guardian*, 12 May 1997, 8–9 (media supplement).

ASTON, M., 'TV for the Masses', *Underground* (Nov. 1987), 12.

BERLAND, JODY, 'Locating Listening: Technological Space, Popular Music, Canadian Mediations', in *Cultural Studies*, 2 (1988), 343–58.

—— 'Radio Space and Industrial Time: Music Formats, Local Narratives and Technological Mediation', in *Popular Music*, 9: 2 (1990), 179–92.

—— 'Sound, Image and Social Space: Music Video and Media Reconstruction', in S. Frith, A. Goodwin, and L. Grossberg (eds.), *Sound & Vision: The Music Video Reader* (London: Routledge, 1993), 25–45.

BRACEWELL, MICHAEL, 'The Clone Zone', *Guardian*, 7 Apr. 1997, 2–3 (media supplement).

BROOKER, CHARLIE, 'Tomb Raider', *PC Zone*, 44 (Nov. 1996), 48–9.

BRUNO, GUILIANA, 'Ramble City: Postmodernism and *BladeRunner*', in A. Kuhn (ed.), *Alien Zone: Cultural Theory and Contemporary Science Fiction Cinema* (London: Verso, 1990), 183–96.

CALDWELL, JOHN T., *Televisuality: Style, Crisis and Authority in American Television* (New Brunswick, NJ: Rutgers University Press, 1995).

CANNON, DAVID, 'Generation X and the New Work Ethic', a Demos working paper (London: Demos, 1994).

COHEN, SARA, 'Localizing Sound', in W. Straw, S. Johnson, R. Sullivan, and P. Friedlander (eds.), *Popular Music—Style and Identity* (Montreal: Centre for Research on Canadian Cultural Industries and Institutions for IASPM, 1995), 61–8.

COHEN, STANLEY, *Folk Devils and Moral Panics: The Creation of the Mods and Rockers* (London: MacGibbon and Kee, 1972).

COLLINS, JIM, 'Post-Modernism as Culmination: The Aesthetic Politics of Decentred Cultures' (1989), reprinted in C. Jencks (ed.), *The Post-Modern Reader* (London: Academy Editions, 1992), 94–119.

—— 'Batman: The Movie, Narrative: the Hyperconscious', in R. Pearson and W. Urrichio (eds.), *The Many Lives of Batman: Critical Approaches to a Superhero and his Media* (London: British Film Industry, 1991), 164–81.

COUPLAND, DOUGLAS, *Generation X: Tales for an Accelerated Culture* (London: Abacus, 1991).

Cubitt, Sean, 'Top of the Pops: The Politics of the Living Room', in L. Masterman (ed.), *Television Mythologies: Stars, Shows and Signs* (London: Comedia/Routledge, 1984), 46–8.

Curran, J., Morley, D., and Walkerdine, V. (eds.), *Cultural Studies and Communications* (London: Arnold, 1996).

D'Agostino, P., and Tafler, D. (eds.), *Transmission: Towards a Post-Television Culture* (London: Sage, 1995).

Dienst, Richard, *Still Life in Real Time: Theory after Television* (Durham, NC, and London: Duke University Press, 1994).

Doane, Mary Ann, 'Information, Crisis, Catastrophe', in P. Mellencamp (ed.), *Logics of Television: Essays in Cultural Criticism* (London: British Film Institute, 1990), 222–39.

Dyer, Richard, *Light Entertainment* (London: British Film Institute, 1973).

Ellis, John, *Visible Fictions: Cinema, Television, Video* (London: Routledge, 1982; revised edition published in 1992).

Featherstone, M., and Burrows, R. (eds.), *Cyberspace, Cyberbodies, Cyberpunk: Cultures of Technological Embodiment* (London: Sage, 1995).

Fiske, John, *Television Culture* (London: Routledge, 1987).

Fornas, Johan, *Cultural Theory & Late Modernity* (London: Sage, 1995).

Frith, Simon, 'Youth/Music/Television', in S. Frith, A. Goodwin, and L. Grossberg (eds.), *Sound & Vision: The Music Video Reader* (London: Routledge, 1993), 67–85.

—— 'Music and Identity', in S. Hall and P. du Gay (eds.), *Questions of Cultural Identity* (London: Sage, 1996), 108–28.

Furlong, Ruth, 'There's No Place Like Home', in M. Lister (ed.), *The Photographic Image in Digital Culture* (London and New York: Routledge, 1995), 170–87.

Garratt, Sheryl, 'Teenage Dreams', in S. Frith and A. Goodwin (eds.), *On Record: Rock, Pop and the Written Word* (New York: Pantheon Books, 1990), 399–409.

Goodwin, Andrew, *Dancing in the Distraction Factory: Music, Television and Popular Culture* (Bloomington, Ind., and Minneapolis: University of Minnesota Press, 1992).

Grossberg, Larry, *We Gotta Get Out of this Place: Popular Conservatism and Postmodern Culture* (London: Routledge, 1992).

—— Nelson, C., and Treichler, P. (eds.), *Cultural Studies* (London and New York: Routledge, 1992).

Handhardt, J. (ed.), *Video Culture: A Critical Investigation* (New York: Gibbs M. Smith, Inc., Peregrine Smith Books, and Visual Studies Workshop, 1986).

Hartley, John, *Tele-ology: Studies in Television* (London and New York: Routledge, 1992).

Harvey, David, *The Condition of Postmodernity* (Oxford: Basil Blackwell, 1989).

Hibbert, Tom, 'What the Hell does *The Word* Think it is?', *Q* (Mar. 1992), 7.

Hill, John, 'Television and Pop: The Case of the 1950s', in J. Corner (ed.), *Popular Television in Britain* (London: British Film Institute, 1991), 90–107.

HORTON, DONALD, and WOHL, R. RICHARD, 'Mass Communication and Para-Social Interaction: Observations on Intimacy at a Distance', *Psychiatry*, 19 (1956), 215–23, excerpted in John Corner and Jeremy Hawthorn (eds.), *Communication Studies: An Introductory Reader* (4th edn., London: Edward Arnold, 1993), 156–65.

JENCKS, C. (ed.), *The Post-Modern Reader* (London: Academy Editions, 1992).

JENKS, CHRIS (ed.), *Visual Culture* (London and New York: Routledge, 1995.)

JOHNSTON, C., 'I Have Snubbed the Future', *Village Voice*, 20 Oct. 1987, 24.

KAPLAN, E. ANN, *Rocking Around the Clock: Music Television, Postmodernism and Consumer Culture* (London: Methuen, 1987).

KROLL, JACK, 'The Heartbreak Kid' (1977), in K. Quain (ed.), *The Elvis Reader: Texts and Sources on the King of Rock'n'Roll* (New York: St Martin's Press, 1992), 68–71.

KUHN, ANNETTE, 'Mandy and Possibility', *Screen*, 33: 3 (Autumn 1992), 233–44.

LEFEBVRE, HENRI, *The Production of Space*, trans. D. Nicholson-Smith (Oxford: Blackwell, 1991).

LEWIS, BILL, 'TV Games: People as Performers', in L. Masterman (ed.), *TV Mythologies* (London: Comedia/Routledge, 1984), 42–5.

LURY, CELIA, *Consumer Culture* (Cambridge: Polity, 1996).

McLELLAN, JIM, 'Down the Tube', *The Face*, 54 (Mar. 1993), 48–53.

MARCUS, GREIL, 'Notes on the Life & Death and Incandescent Banality of Rock'n'Roll' (1992), reprinted in H. Kureshi and J. Savage (eds.), *The Faber Book of Pop* (London: Faber and Faber, 1995), 739–53.

MASSEY, DOREEN, *Space, Place and Gender* (Cambridge: Polity Press, 1994).

MELLENCAMP, PATRICIA, 'TV Time and Catastrophe, or *Beyond the Pleasure Principle* of Television', in P. Mellencamp (ed.), *Logics of Television: Essays in Cultural Criticism* (London: British Film Institute, 1990), 240–66.

MORLEY, DAVID, and ROBINS, KEVIN, *Spaces of Identity: Global Media, Electronic Landscapes and Cultural Boundaries* (London: Routledge, 1995).

MORSE, MARGARET, 'An Ontology of Everyday Distraction: The Freeway, the Mall, and Television', in P. Mellencamp (ed.), *Logics of Television: Essays in Cultural Criticism* (London: British Film Institute, 1990), 193–222.

—— 'Television Graphics and the Virtual Body: Words on the Move', in Margaret Morse, *Virtualities: Television, Media Art and Cyberculture* (Bloomington, Ind.: Indiana University Press, 1998).

NEWCOMB, H. (ed.), *Television: The Critical View* (New York and Oxford: Oxford University Press, 1994).

O'KELLY, LISA, 'Youngsters Just Wanna Have Fun', *Independent*, 22 July 1992, 15.

ORTH, MAUREEN, 'All Shook Up' (1977), in K. Quain (ed.), *The Elvis Reader: Texts and Sources on the King of Rock'n'Roll* (New York: St Martin's Press, 1992), 63–7.

RADEN, BILL, 'I Want my *Snub TV*', *Los Angeles Times*, 17 Oct. 1987, 16.

ROBINS, KEVIN, 'Will Images Move Us Still?', in M. Lister (ed.), *The Photographic Image in Digital Culture* (London and New York: Routledge, 1995), 29–50.

Ross, A., and Rose, T. (eds.), *Microphone Fiends: Youth Music, Youth Culture* (New York and London: Routledge, 1994).

Rushkoff, Douglas, 'On the Guess List', *Guardian*, 16 Jan. 1997, 7 (on-line supplement).

Scannell, Paddy, *Radio, Television and Modern Life: A Phenomenological Approach* (Oxford: Blackwell, 1996).

Screen, Special Issue: Postmodern Screen, 28: 2 (1987).

Shearman, Colin, 'More Pop and Less Champagne', *Guardian*, 23 Mar. 1989, 28.

Silverstone, Roger, *Television and Everyday Life* (London and New York: Routledge, 1994).

—— and Hirsch, Eric (eds.), *Consuming Technologies: Media and Information in Domestic Spaces* (London and New York: Routledge, 1994).

Skelton, Tracey, and Valentine, Gill (eds.), *Cool Places: Geographies of Youth Cultures* (London: Routledge, 1998).

Skirrow, Gillian, 'Women/Acting/Power', in H. Baehr and G. Dyer (eds.), *Boxed In: Women and Television* (London: Pandora Press, 1987), 164–84.

—— 'Hellivision: An Analysis of Video Games', reprinted in M. Alvarado and J. O. Thompson (eds.), *The Media Reader* (London: British Film Institute, 1990), 321–38.

Slater, Don, 'Domestic Photography and Digital Culture', in M. Lister (ed.), *The Photographic Image in Digital Culture* (London: Routledge, 1995), 129–47.

Stallabrass, Julian, 'Just Gaming: Allegory and Economy in Computer Games', *New Left Review*, 198 (1993), 83–107.

Sterling, Bruce (ed.), *Mirrorshades: The Cyberpunk Anthology* (London: Paladin, 1986, paperback 1988), pp. vii–xiv.

Stoddart, Patrick, 'A Rough Guide to the Streetwise', *Observer*, 17 Aug. 1988, 20.

Taussig, Michael, *The Nervous System* (London and New York: Routledge, 1992).

Thornton, Sarah, *Club Cultures: Music, Media and Sub-Cultural Capital* (Cambridge: Polity Press, 1995).

Tolson, Andrew, *Mediations: Text and Discourse in Media Studies* (London: Edward Arnold, 1996).

Turkle, Sherry, *The Second Self: Computers and the Human Spirit* (New York: Simon and Schuster, 1984).

—— *Life on the Screen: Identity in the Age of the Internet* (London: Weidenfeld & Nicolson, 1996).

Waters, John, 'The Nicest Kids in Town', reprinted in H. Kureshi and J. Savage (eds.), *The Faber Book of Pop* (London: Faber and Faber, 1995), 152–8.

Whannel, Garry, 'Winner Takes All: Competition', in A. Goodwin and G. Whannel (eds.), *Understanding Television* (London and New York: Routledge, 1990), 103–14.

Wheale, N. (ed.), *Postmodern Arts* (London and New York: Routledge, 1995).

WILLIAMS, RAYMOND, *Television: Technology and Cultural Form* (New York and London: Routledge, 1974; republished 1994).

WILLIS, PAUL, *Moving Culture* (London: Calouste Gulbenkian Foundation, 1990).

WURTZLER, STEVE, 'She Sang Live, but the Microphone was Turned Off: The Live, the Recorded and the *Subject* of Representation', in R. Altman (ed.), *Sound Theory, Sound Practice* (New York and London: Routledge, 1992), 87–103.

ZIEHE, THOMAS, 'Cultural Modernity and Individualisation: Changed Symbolic Contexts for Young People', in J. Fornas and G. Bolin (eds.), *Moves in Modernity* (Stockholm: Almqvist & Wiskell, 1992), 73–103.

Index